America and Europe
in an Era of Change

America and Europe in an Era of Change

EDITED BY
Helga Haftendorn and Christian Tuschhoff

Westview Press

BOULDER • SAN FRANCISCO • OXFORD

Copyright © 1993 by Westview Press, Inc.

Published in 1993 in the United States of America by Westview Press, Inc., 5500 Central Avenue, Boulder, Colorado 80301-2877, and in the United Kingdom by Westview Press, 36 Lonsdale Road, Summertown, Oxford OX2 7EW

Library of Congress Cataloging-in-Publication Data
America and Europe in an era of change / edited by Helga Haftendorn
  and Christian Tuschhoff.
    p. cm.
  Includes bibliographical references and index.
  ISBN 0-8133-1670-7. — ISBN 0-8133-1671-5 (pbk.)
  1. Europe—Foreign relations—United States. 2. United States—
Foreign relations—Europe. 3. World politics—1989–
I. Haftendorn, Helga. II. Tuschhoff, Christian, 1955– .
D1064.U5A79 1993
909'.098210829—dc20   92-31017
                                                                          CIP

Printed and bound in the United States of America

The paper used in this publication meets the requirements of the American National Standard for Permanence of Paper for Printed Library Materials Z39.48-1984.

10 9 8 7 6 5 4 3 2 1

Contents

Tables

Preface

In early 1990, the John F. Kennedy Institute of American Studies and the Institute of International Relations and Regional Studies of the Free University in Berlin asked a number of prominent U.S. scholars to elaborate their views on "America and Europe in an Era of Change." The occasion was the institutes' annual Ernst Fraenkel Lecture Series, held during the academic year 1990–1991 in memory of late German-American political scientist Ernst Fraenkel. Each speaker was asked to analyze the roles of America and Europe, in the global system and vis-à-vis each other, before the background of the revolutionary changes we are witnessing in international affairs, by using his or her analytical "lenses." These presentations were revised and to some extent expanded by the authors to form the background of the following chapters. Given the speed of changes in what was formerly the Soviet Union, some of the most recent developments could not be integrated into this volume.

The result is, as the editors feel, a most significant and timely description of the role of America and Europe in an era of change, as the title of this volume signals. The high level of theoretical reflection of most, if not all, chapters ensures that our authors' analyses will endure even if some of the factors analyzed have further evolved.

This volume owes much to the cooperation of each individual author and to the generous assistance by a number of persons and institutions. Many thanks go to the Fritz Thyssen Foundation and Jürgen Christian Regge for funding as well as to the John F. Kennedy Institute and Professor Carl Ludwig Holtfrerich for co-hosting the Ernst Fraenkel Lecture Series. The Ernst Reuter Foundation with its *spiritus rector* Dr. Horst Hartwich has provided funds for the publication of this volume, and Heidi Strecker has been a very committed and efficient copy editor. Thanks are further due to Jennifer Knerr, Libby Barstow, and Sarah Tomasek of Westview Press, who provided professional help throughout the process of publishing. The lecture series and volume would not have been possible, however, without the support from our colleagues and the logistics of the Center for Transatlantic Foreign and Security Policy Studies of the Free University of Berlin. It is with gratitude that the editors recognize all the assistance they have received.

Helga Haftendorn
Christian Tuschhoff

1

Causes and Consequences of Change: Contending Approaches and Competing Perspectives

Helga Haftendorn and Christian Tuschhoff

ANALYZING CHANGE IN
THE INTERNATIONAL SYSTEM

The faltering of the Soviet Union, the disintegration of the once monolithic Communist bloc, the end of the Cold War, and the reunification of Germany and Europe signify the most radical changes in the political map of Europe since the end of World War II. Impressed by the magnitude of this transformation of the international system, Francis Fukuyama suggests that it signifies "the end of history."[1] In comparison to what is happening in the East, the changes within the West seem quite small and rather subtle. But there are changes, most visibly in the capabilities, roles, and policies of both Western Europe and the United States. To some extent they are the result of political and economic reconstruction in Europe as well as of a normalization in the international role of America—less "world policeman" and more "ordinary country."[2]

Relations between Europe and America are also changing, as a reaction to the revolutionary events in East and Central Europe and in the international system as such and as a result of the transformation of the potentials of both. Within the bipolar structure of East-West competition, Europe had been the focus of attention and the prize for which the United States and the Soviet Union competed. With the end of the Cold War, Europe has lost this relational relevance and definitely its primacy for the United States. Its weight now depends on its indigenous capabilities, and it has to compete for attention with other states and regions that have gained in importance. It is significant that most of our American authors who were asked to focus on America and Europe also mention Japan and compare its role to that of Europe or Germany.

But neither causes nor consequences of the changing relationship between Europe and America are yet clearly established. How seriously should we take the "declinists'" argument[3] that America, because of imperial overstretch, has lost its competitive edge to Japan and possibly also to the European Community (EC)? Has the primarily patron-client relationship between the United States and West Europe eroded and given way to a new "partnership in leadership"?[4] Or does the European-American relationship merely mirror the new complexities of international interdependence?

This book assembles a group of distinguished American scholars to describe, explain, and predict further the change in the transatlantic relationship. The authors were asked to present their views of the causes and consequences of change by, first, using their specific analytical lenses that rest upon their individual theoretical frameworks and, second, by addressing the following questions:

- How did the structure of the international system change and what probable consequences can we expect?
- Is a structural change better described as a change of the balance of power among states, as a change of the currencies of power, or as a combination of both?
- How do international institutions change and what will be the effects?
- How does the international agenda of the most urgent problems and policies change and can we expect more conflict or more cooperation?

In addition to responding to these questions, which focus on the causes of change, all authors were expected to comment on some consequences for the behavior of states by addressing the following questions:

- Who are the winners and losers of international change?
- What will be the new roles and policies of states on both sides of the Atlantic? Will they result in a new division of labor?

THE EMERGING STRUCTURE OF
THE INTERNATIONAL SYSTEM:
POLARITY, CAKE, OR CONCERT?

With respect to the international system, the term *structure* refers to the ordering of principles as well as to the distribution of capabilities among units that leads to various forms of polarity. Although none of the authors question the endurance of anarchy[5] in international relations, their assessment of the distribution of capabilities and its impact on transatlantic relations varies considerably.

Stephen D. Krasner adopts a realist perspective in Chapter 2 by asserting that "the range of options available to any state is constrained by the international distribution of power." He looks not only at the transformation of the relationship among the superpowers but also at that between the United States and its allies. The distribution of power between the United States and the Soviet Union has changed from bipolarity to unipolarity. Soviet power has been overestimated in the past and is faltering in the present. The balances between the United States and its allies have changed from a highly hierarchical to a more equal distribution of capabilities as Japan and Germany have gained considerably in economic power. As a consequence, the range of foreign policy options available to countries has changed as well. The range of options available to the United States has narrowed, whereas European states and Japan may now select among a much wider range of options.

Joseph S. Nye, Jr., and Robert O. Keohane maintain that neither the Soviet Union nor Russia as its successor will be able to sustain a superpower status. It may, however, remain a great power because it produces the largest share of oil in the world and has vast natural resources, a large educated population, and nuclear weapons at its disposal. Thus the Soviet decline causes the end of bipolarity. But what kind of new structure will emerge in the post–Cold War era?

Peter J. Katzenstein argues that the existing international structure will be complemented by political regionalism: the values, interests, and political institutions by which decisionmakers define their foreign policy goals. In specific regional environments, states feel comfortable to pursue their domestic and foreign agendas. Katzenstein predicts that three different regions will emerge: America, Asia, and Europe. A new regionalism might lead to a system of three power blocs somewhat similar to Keohane's tripolar structure of the world political economy, which consists of Europe, America, and Japan.

However, in Chapter 6 Nye opposes the notion of regional blocs because (1) strong transnational forces will resist fragmentation and regionalization and (2) residual national interests will prevent large-scale regional integration. He instead proposes an image of the international system as a layer cake in which "the Americans predominate in the top military layer, the economic middle layer is multipolar (and has been for two decades), and the bottom layer of transnational interdependence is characterized by a diffusion of power." Depending on the specific issue area, the international system takes on not a single form but diverse forms ranging from unipolarity to multipolarity. According to both Katzenstein and Nye, the present and likely future distribution of capabilities will generate a sufficient degree of regional and international stability.

But how will emerging regions such as Europe be organized? Richard N. Rosecrance provides a unique answer. According to him, the future international system will consist of communities of actors arranged in concentric circles around a core. Rather than evolving into a nineteenth-century–style power system consisting of self-assertive nation-states, the international system will possibly consist of an even stronger concert of nations supplemented by regional institutions.

The stability of the international system will depend on the cohesion of the core, which he believes will be Europe. For the first time in history, this European core will hold together, for three reasons. First, no key actor has the option of isolationism. Second, economic interdependence supports the cohesiveness of the core, as states have great stakes in the prosperity of each other. The components of interdependence, one might add, will lead to mutual recognition that continued cooperation within the European Community and permanent adjustment of its institutions are preferable to renationalization. Third, the European core will draw other countries into its orbit rather than stimulate the emergence of another powerful core to counterbalance this system, as realists would predict. Each unit within the system retains some degree of autonomy and national independence, as there is no central political decisionmaking body. The new concert is stable even under the threat of new trading blocs because changes in the concert are managed through peaceful trade rather than war. For enduring cooperation, Rosecrance argues, direct investment is even more important than trade. With high foreign investment, the stakes countries have in each others' economy are maintained.

Although the political order in Europe will largely depend on the role of European organizations, these institutions are themselves subject to far-reaching changes. This raises the question of how changing international institutions affect state action.

CHANGING INTERNATIONAL INSTITUTIONS AND THEIR CONSEQUENCES FOR STATE ACTION

In Chapter 3, Keohane takes a middle position between Katzenstein and Nye. Like Katzenstein, Keohane sees a "tripolar" world emerging in the international political economy. But he also agrees with Nye on both the importance of international institutions in an interdependent environment and on the need for U.S. leadership to maintain the stability of the international system. International institutions will be particularly helpful because "they are more responsive to human action than either fundamental political tendencies such as hypernationalism or the international political structures of bipolarity or multipolarity."

p.53

Keohane and Nye thus reject Krasner's argument that the range of foreign policy options available to the United States has been restricted by a decline of resources. The United States, they believe, is the only remaining superpower and will therefore be able to control outcomes by manipulating international institutions.

They maintain that international institutions can be built and altered according to changing requirements of stability. Institutions contribute to stability as they modify the behavior of states from striving for relative gains to seeking absolute ones. Institutions also allow the United States to exercise world leadership. Because neither Japan nor Europe appears capable of assuming global responsibility, the United States will have to continue carrying this burden.

But how do actors cope with the changing nature and increasing complexity of international politics? Katzenstein, on the one hand, and Keohane and Nye, on the other, refer to different settings that induce states and other actors to reduce complexity, define problems, and formulate policies. Whereas Katzenstein believes that regions will play a mediating role between the demands of the international system and domestic politics, Nye and Keohane emphasize the need to develop and strengthen multilateral institutions to assist governments in finding their way through the jungle of increasingly complex international relations. Institutions, Nye argues, shape an actor's expectations on probabilities of outcomes. They can facilitate information exchange, contribute to burden sharing, promote diplomatic activities, and establish rules and procedures to provide for continuity. However, other factors will also change and thereby affect the existing balance of power.

CHANGING CURRENCIES OF POWER

Contributors to this volume do not agree that a "balance of power" exists. Some instead prefer to speak of a "distribution of capabilities." In our context, the semantic difference is insignificant because both concepts refer to outcomes such as stability and peaceful change in the international system. Hence both terms can be used interchangeably although one needs to be reminded that they have different implications within a larger theoretical framework. The term "currencies of power" refers to the military, economic, political, and ideological instruments that impact on an actor's ability to pursue foreign policy goals. The main question is if and how changes in the relative importance of one or more instruments affect policy outcomes.

There is wide agreement that, as Krasner and Keohane argue, in the future the main instruments of power and leverage will be economic rather than military. Economic instruments for coercive action as well as for conflict resolution notwithstanding, Krasner, Rosecrance, and others emphasize that nuclear weapons still play a predominant role in maintaining what John L. Gaddis calls "the long peace"[6] and will continue to be the bedrock of international stability. However, they are inadequate to offset imbalances that are likely to lead to conflict short of war. The management of conflicts increasingly requires reliance on instruments other than military.

Major changes in the means of conflict resolution also affect the existing distribution of capabilities among states in pursuit of foreign policies. The central question is whether the middle layer of Nye's three-layer cake—economics—will gain in importance and thus supersede the military layer in which the United States still plays a predominant role. Furthermore, will such a shift in the currencies of power also affect the distribution of capabilities among states? And if so, what is the likely impact on the distribution of responsibilities among actors for maintaining a stable international system?

In answering these questions our authors make competing predictions. Those arguing for a sweeping change in the distribution of capabilities normally refer to economic indicators. According to Katzenstein, the shift in power from the United States to Asia is most visible in capital markets. Japanese firms also enjoy a substantial lead across the board in all areas of industrial production. Japan's technological dynamics thus foreshadow a fundamental shift in political and military relations in the decades to come.

In Chapter 2, Krasner goes one step further in his analysis than did Katzenstein and visualizes the United States in decline. The power of the United States has diminished, which has led to a relative weakening of its international position. This process was most visible from the late 1940s until about 1970. Krasner concludes that Soviet power has for years been both overestimated and in decline. In contrast, Japan and united Germany have been the great winners. As a consequence, the world has moved "from a period of American hegemony . . . to a period in which the distribution of power is, paradoxically, more unipolar but less hierarchical."

Krasner predicts that the changing balance of power will also lead to a transformation of the distribution in relative responsibilities by each state for preserving the stability of the international system. According to him, Europe should carry a larger burden and look after its own defense. However, "if the European Community does become an effective political and security entity, then the Atlantic Alliance . . . is finished." The United States will continue to play its role as an honest broker only "if the community fails to develop an integrated security and foreign policy." Krasner believes that other actors will fill the gap if the United States in the future is unable to execute its leadership or if this leadership is relatively unimportant. The stability of the international system, however, will not be at risk.

Nye argues the opposite case in Chapter 6. He strongly disputes that the power of the United States has declined. He disagrees with Krasner's analysis of negative trends in the American economy and, together with Keohane, opposes Krasner's argument that U.S. leadership will increasingly be superfluous. He explains the loss in international influence as a process of "normalization" after the extraordinary American predominance after World War II. Pessimistic assessments of U.S. power are flawed because they are based upon a comparison of "the bad in the present with the good in the past." The United States has never been able to turn its overwhelming power into influence over friends or foes. Nye concedes that a loss of U.S. influence resulted from a process of growing international interdependence and a diffusion of power. Both, however, do not constitute a decline of the power resources the United States still has at its disposal. It will be able to continuously provide for strong world leadership as a precondition of international stability.

With regard to the changing balance of power and its impact on the United States, Stanley Hoffmann writes in Chapter 4 that the emerging unipolarity is paradoxical because the United States can no longer rely on two major instruments of its foreign policy—eco-

nomic assistance and arms sales. Its diplomatic activism since the
Gulf War has been nothing but a "shrewd attempt at exploiting the
image of a victorious great power." However, the growing engagement of the United States in multilateral diplomacy can also be
interpreted as a smart attempt to withdraw some of the political
investments (including accumulated interest) that after World War
II served to reconstruct Europe and shift them to other geographical
areas. Taking the lead in multilateral diplomacy does not necessarily
require that a country have its own resources but that it have the
ability to make use of the comparative advantages of other countries. Keohane has in mind precisely this "soft power" (as described
by Nye) of using multilateral institutions when he advocates global
U.S. leadership to maintain stability in the international system.

In sum, although the authors disagree on whether changing currencies of power affect the stability of the international system,
almost all agree that such changes will have a deep impact on both
the distribution of responsibilities among states and the roles that
actors will play in the future.

SHIFTS IN THE AGENDA OF
INTERNATIONAL RELATIONS

The reduced emphasis on the military as a means to achieve
security opened up an academic debate on "new dimensions of
security."[7] This debate focuses on the lessons to be drawn from
history. Different historic experiences shape different sets of values
and norms of how to pursue foreign policy goals in a changing
international environment. The United States, Japan, and Germany
present unique models of how to define security and how to set an
agenda for international relations, as Katzenstein observes. The globally prevailing model will reward its promoter by providing it with
a "competitive advantage."[8] The competition between the regions
will therefore essentially be a conflict over the dominant agenda.

An illustration of the fundamental difference in the evaluation of
the military can be found in Krasner's and Katzenstein's analyses
of the Gulf War. Each analysis is based on different assumptions.
Given his realist premises, Krasner wonders why the least oil-de-
pendent countries (the United States and Great Britain) deployed the
largest military contingents to liberate Kuwait whereas the most
energy-dependent state (Japan) sent none at all. He concludes that
"something is wrong here" with Japan taking a free ride. From a
comparative perspective, Katzenstein explains that Japan preferred

a diplomatic solution to a military solution because it could economically afford to pay almost any price for oil. Whereas the United States tends to look at security from a military perspective, Japan approaches it from an economic point of view. This difference is a perfect example of how the same issue is defined according to either a military or an economic frame of reference and thus leads to different political actions. The case also illustrates that how an issue is defined determines the distribution of comparative advantages among the actors involved.

What will, then, be the predominant agenda in international relations? Can we expect more conflict or more cooperation? Katzenstein offers an optimistic outlook for the twenty-first century. He believes that all three regions will give important impulses to the international system: America will provide for the multicultural experiment, Europe will promote the model of an industrial society compatible with environmental protection, and Asia will develop innovative technologies for the development and marketing of goods. Katzenstein seems to imply a fundamental compatibility of these impulses. Hence one might expect that cooperation among regions will be the prevailing pattern of behavior. However, does such a division of labor among regions provide for global stability? A less optimistic outlook starts from the assumption that the three impulses are not necessarily compatible with each other. Instead, they will compete to attain top priority on the global agenda. Thus Katzenstein's division of labor among regions might lead to a fundamental conflict of interests. The main beneficiary of change will be the region whose impulse will prevail.

A conflict of interests will likely remain the predominant pattern of transatlantic relations. Hoffmann maintains that economic competition between the United States and Europe will continue. Nevertheless, the common bond of security issues will remain on top of the transatlantic agenda. Here Catherine M. Kelleher and Robert D. Putnam disagree. Kelleher believes that given a diminished importance of the U.S. troop presence in Europe, military issues will lose their paramount importance. They will be replaced by an intensification of diplomatic exchanges. Putnam predicts that security issues will become less divisive and conflicts over security will concern less vital interests. He assumes that the Atlantic Alliance will be more stable the fewer conflicts on crucial issues it has to cope with. Because remaining conflicts concern less vital issues, transatlantic relations will be more stable.

What, however, is the purpose and the justification for an alliance if the stakes are less then vital? Would the North Atlantic Treaty

Organization (NATO) then be less important for balancing interests, risks, and responsibilities of all partners? Hoffmann predicts in Chapter 4 that a "combination of economic inequities and ethnic or religious grievances" will dominate the international agenda. Western Europe, rather than the United States, will engage in the economic and political reconstruction of Eastern Europe and the Soviet Union. A shift of emphasis from transatlantic cooperation to intra-European affairs could further contribute to a weakening of relations between Western Europe and the United States.

In sum, most authors in this volume agree that the structure of the international system—which includes its polarity, international institutions, currencies of power, and agenda shifts—has changed, yet some disagreement remains. First, they disagree on how structures have changed. Second, they disagree on the relative significance of the various changes (e.g., does a shift from bipolarity to unipolarity change the behavior of actors in a more fundamental way than a change of international institutions?). We should not expect authors to produce a consensus because the answer depends upon the theoretical assumptions underlying each statement.

WINNERS AND LOSERS IN
INTERNATIONAL POLITICS

After fifty years of Cold War it is evident that the United States has been more successful than expected in building modern societies in Europe and Asia that are "like us," as Kelleher has termed it in Chapter 9. Katzenstein argues that by assisting the Japanese and the Germans in the reconstruction of their socioeconomic systems after World War II, the United States planted competitors in the international system that are better equipped institutionally to cope with the challenges of the future than is the United States itself. The success of the reconstruction of Europe could thus result in American setbacks. If, in fact, history moves in long cycles of rise and decline of powers, one wonders what lessons Western policymakers assisting the reform of Eastern Europe should draw from this fact. Might they not hesitate to modernize East European societies that in the long run could turn into powerful competitors of Western Europe because they are better adjusted institutionally to new international challenges?

Krasner argues that a new balance of power—the United States vis-à-vis Europe—will lead to a redistribution of responsibilities among actors such as maintaining international stability or European security, though states are still too reluctant to adapt to the new realities. In Chapter 2 he writes that "the United States is still doing too much, and Japan and Germany (or perhaps Europe as a whole) are doing too little." He predicts that U.S. policies will turn more inward. Given the relative shortage of resources, the United States will no longer be able to pursue what Krasner calls "milieu goals," that is, the promotion of an international environment consisting of countries that Americans feel are like America. Rather, the United States will actively follow narrowly defined economic and political interests. In contrast, before the 1970s it was concerned with global stability and based its policy on reciprocity, openness, and nondiscrimination.

According to Krasner, the United States has changed its policies in response to its decline in power but has not yet found a new strategic vision. In Chapter 2, Krasner writes that U.S. "foreign economic policy so far has not been marked by the replacement of one set of principles by another but rather by the accretion of one set of practices on top of other earlier practices that might have been based on different principles and norms." As the United States loses leverage on its allies, policy coordination becomes more difficult. Coercive bargaining (which Krasner assumes is inconsistent with the broader principle of free trade) could be used to enforce free market rules. He sees the United States gradually drifting away from its former responsibility for global order based on the principles it established after World War II. In short, because the United States is the main loser from structural change in international politics, it is bound to adjust its foreign policy behavior.

Krasner and Nye disagree on the implications of this process of "decline" or "normalization" of U.S. power. Krasner argues that the United States inevitably must give up some of its responsibilities, whereas Nye, together with Keohane, claims that the United States is "bound to lead" because no other state is both willing and qualified to assume an active global leadership role. Moreover, the United States remains the greatest power of the world and continues to be the main beneficiary of this order. It can afford global leadership given the vast resources at its disposal. Keohane adds that the United States still commands the power to manipulate international institutions, which is necessary for maintaining global leadership.

Hoffmann observes that there is an undercurrent of disorientation in the United States resulting from U.S. difficulties in translating military power into political success. Because economic problems such as huge budget and trade deficits preclude the application of the usual economic instruments in foreign policy, the United States is shifting its priorities to domestic issues to underscore its position in the world. Hoffmann suggests that in the short term there will be a change in U.S. foreign policy from an active to a more passive behavior. However, after a period of domestic consolidation the United States could move back to a more active foreign policy.

Krasner, Keohane, and Nye agree, however, that so far neither Japan nor Europe has taken over global responsibilities for the maintenance of a liberal world order, though these authors disagree on the desirability of such an outcome. What are the chances that Japan or a Europe led by united Germany will commit itself to global leadership in the future? The main winners from recent changes in the international balance of power according to Katzenstein—Germany and Japan—continue to be constrained by a lack of political imagination or interest in military affairs and, with regard to Germany, by deep fissures in political culture. Given these constraints, it is improbable that either Japan or Germany will take over some of the old American responsibilities for maintaining global order. However, they will pursue active foreign policies to build and maintain regional stability in Asia and Europe respectively.

Regardless of its future global role, Europe might lead the process of extending universal principles to Eastern Europe and to what remains of the Soviet Union. Two conditions have to be met, however. First, to pursue common European policies in support of certain principles, the European Community needs to create an efficient foreign policy decisionmaking process by deepening its integrated institutions. Second, to take over responsibility for a common European order the community has to pursue milieu goals, in particular toward its neighbors in the East. The notion of enlargement of the community refers to this second condition. Hence, although it is unlikely that Europe will take over new responsibilities for international stability, it probably will pursue a more active policy to both deepen the process of European integration and broaden other countries' participation.

Both goals are not of equal importance and could be followed as alternative strategies. For Rosecrance, the need to integrate other countries into the European Community is more urgent than the need to deepen the relationship among West Europeans. He is more interested in the effects that the process of broadening has on the countries that are excluded. Even if the Community grows in both population and power, he argues, there is no need to counterbalance it because it does not present a threat. The losers will not feel compelled to align against the winners but will rather pursue a bandwagon strategy. Widening the European Community is likely to produce more regional stability.

Putnam agrees with Rosecrance on the structure of a new concert in Europe. However, Putnam assumes that policy outcomes will depend on both international and domestic factors. Given the complexity of world politics, the interplay among the various actors will increase in importance because it will not always be possible to distribute costs and benefits in an equal and just manner. Putnam suggests that if gains from international cooperation are widespread but costs are concentrated on a small group of actors, cooperation will fail. Interest groups will block complicated international agreements because they feel disproportionately burdened. The demand on the political system to provide for collective goods gets more complicated as nongovernmental actors organize or align themselves across national boundaries—a pattern Putnam calls in Chapter 5 the "consequence of the mismatch between global economics and parochial politics." Thus, global and regional stability through cooperation among states will also depend on an even more complicated game at two tables. It is still too early to predict whether this game can be won. To a considerable degree success depends on the power of national governments to make decisions of fundamental consequences and to domestically enforce international agreements.

With regard to adjusting U.S. domestic politics to a changing international environment, Katzenstein, Putnam, and Kelleher concur that American domestic politics is relatively unaccustomed to policy choices of fundamental consequences and that it instead proceeds incrementally. Putnam recommends strengthening the role of political leaders to enable governments to achieve international agreements that provide for mutually beneficial cooperation. New institutions and leadership arrangements need to be legitimized by appropriate bodies.

ROLES, POLICIES, AND
A NEW DIVISION OF LABOR

Putnam reports that though a majority of Americans blame themselves for their domestic failures, only a few want to abdicate world leadership and return to isolationism. But the United States is neither prepared nor able to continue playing a role as a world hegemon given the growth of interdependence and economic multipolarity. Alhough concurring with Putnam that state power depends, among other factors, upon an actor's "willingness to spend resources on foreign policy" (Keohane, Chapter 3), Keohane and Nye take this intent for granted. However, they do not distinguish strictly between explanatory and prescriptive arguments. In their analyses, Katzenstein and Krasner are less confident than Keohane and Nye that the American political system provides the necessary underpinnings for the willingness of the United States to spend resources on foreign policy. Katzenstein reminds us that the United States is restricted by the inability of its political system to make decisions of fundamental consequences. Most authors agree in their prescriptions, however, that the United States should adhere to its global leadership role because the United States provides for most of the world's collective goods and is also the biggest beneficiary. However, Putnam and Nye expect its role to change from a "command-style leadership to a more subtle behavior—from 'uncle' to 'cousin' " (Putnam, Chapter 5).

Nye and Keohane suggest that the United States and Europe must join in defining problems and making decisions through common institutions. In Chapter 3 Keohane writes, "In my view, U.S. policy needs to use international institutions to achieve any policy departures if not anything so grand as a 'new world order.'" As critics[9] charge, Keohane's recommendation to build and control international institutions is merely a sophisticated way for the United States to achieve relative gains. These critics argue that transnational interdependence and the diffusion of power to small states and nonstate actors place an even heavier burden on the one remaining superpower to take the lead by forming coalitions and developing institutions to foster international stability. Because stability is of overwhelming concern to the United States, Nye and Kelleher agree that strengthening the European Community by both deepening integration and widening its geographical scope is in the interest of the United States. Even if Europe becomes a stronger competitor, the benefits will outweigh the costs for the United States.

It is an open question whether America is able to pursue a foreign policy based exclusively upon macroeconomic cost-benefit calculations. To play a stabilizing role as a persuasive rather than commanding world leader in a multilayered structure might be too heavy a burden for the United States to carry. "Creating and resisting linkages between issues" is, according to Katzenstein, the "art of the power game" that the United States is ill suited to play because of domestic reasons. The United States is constitutionally unable to cope with increased international complexity because it shies away from fundamental policy decisions. For making domestic politics compatible with the goal of maintaining international stability, Katzenstein and Nye rely on different devices: Katzenstein refers to a division of labor within regions, which should provide distinct but mutually reinforcing impulses, whereas Nye expects that international institutions will provide the necessary link by facilitating cooperation. The difference is one of geographical scope rather than of function. Nye believes that global institutions affect states' decisions directly without regional mediation. For Katzenstein, international stability is supported by a fruitful competition and division of labor among America, Asia, and Europe.

Policies of international cooperation need to be based on a domestic consensus. Putnam uses the term "domestic ratification" of international agreements.[10] This concept is preferable to the concept of "domestic constraint" because the bargaining process at both the domestic table and the international table may lead to results not envisaged before. It can open up opportunities to realize "synergistic gains at both tables" (consisting of issue linkages and trade-offs that go beyond originally defined "win-sets" of minimum foreign policy goals). Bargaining is a much more dynamic and therefore less predictable process that can lead to innovative outcomes.

Confidence in bargaining processes may not be sufficient to achieve international stability. Fundamental adjustments of foreign policies on both sides of the Atlantic will also be required. Eventually, they might lead to a new division of labor between the United States and Europe. Kelleher is concerned with security in general and military issues in particular. Building a European defense identity is a driving force behind the modification of both national foreign policies and decisionmaking procedures within the EC. Kelleher is confident that the United States will continue to have both interests and stakes in Europe, including (1) to maintain and expand the European security zone, (2) to preserve for itself a role as a major actor in Europe, (3) to manage the orderly political transition of a united Germany and the Soviet Union to their new roles, and (4) to further guarantee political and economic access to Europe after 1992.

Kelleher argues for a continued U.S. commitment outside the American hemisphere, even though she is aware of its costs and the related domestic price tag. Given this essential interest in European affairs, "fundamental changes in American security policy and practice" are required. Adjustments include the way the United States views Europe, its willingness to share in more cooperative decisionmaking arrangements, and a reappraisal of the domestic preconditions for U.S. foreign policy behavior. Kelleher asks for a more flexible policy and a broader vision to guide the fundamental transformation of transatlantic relations into a more symmetrical partnership based on political and economic, rather than military, interests. Thus, she asks for gradual adjustments rather than for swift or fundamental changes of policies on both sides.

None of the contributors to this volume argue for substantial modifications of U.S. domestic institutions, though both Kelleher and Katzenstein observe that these institutions might not be particularly suitable for reacting swiftly to fundamental changes. With increased international interdependence, however, it is highly unlikely that any state will be able to maintain autonomous institutional arrangements that are inconsistent with those of other countries. In Europe, the "Europeanization" of rules and regulations that constitute national legal, financial, economic, and political subsystems are transformed by the process of integration. This process does not stop at water's edge but will require corresponding adjustments by the United States not only of policies but also of national institutions.

Kelleher summarizes the challenges to Europe and the United States: First, Europe demands a defense identity of its own, "one in which there will be new borders of identity and new partnerships." Second, given the diminishing threat from the East, the new Europe will have considerably lower military requirements. Third, the Western powers need to revise their relationship with Germany—"the key actor in all the future European circles." Fourth, the United States is tied "to security concerns and arrangements in Europe by interest and convenience" and less so by daily necessity. And finally, in sharp contrast to prior perceptions, the United States will have to realize that Europe is only "somewhat like us" (the United States).

NOTES

1. Francis Fukuyama, "The End of History?" *National Interest,* no. 16 (Summer 1989), pp. 3–18. See also his "The End of History Is Still Nigh," in *The Independent,* March 3, 1992.

2. Richard Rosecrance, ed., *America as an Ordinary Country: U.S. Foreign Policy and the Future* (Ithaca, N.Y.: Cornell University Press 1976).

3. This debate was started by Paul Kennedy with his seminal work *The Rise and Fall of the Great Powers: Economic Change and Military Conflict from 1500 to 2000* (New York: Random House 1967). He has been joined, among others, by Davis P. Calleo, *Beyond American Hegemony: The Future of the Western Alliance* (New York: Basic Books 1987), and rebutted by Samuel P. Huntington, "The U.S.–Decline or Renewal," *Foreign Affairs* 67, no. 2 (Winter 1988/89), pp. 76–6; Henry R. Nau, *The Myth of America's Decline: Leading the World Economy into the 1990s* (New York and Oxford:

Oxford University Press 1990); Joseph S. Nye, Jr., *Bound to Lead: The Changing Nature of American Power* (New York: Basic Books 1990).

4. Address by President George Bush in Mayence, May 31, 1989, *U.S. Policy Information and Texts,* no. 70, Bonn, June 1, 1989.

5. Robert O. Keohane, however, argues in Chapter 3 that the "absence of a centralized enforcement power on a global basis" explains neither cooperation nor conflict among states. Whereas "anarchy . . . has been constant through the history of the interstate system," he says, "cooperation among states has varied substantially."

6. John L. Gaddis, "The Long Peace: Elements of Stability in the Postwar International System," *International Security* 10, no. 4 (Spring 1986), pp. 99–142.

7. Joseph S. Nye, Jr., and Sean M. Lynn-Jones, "International Security Studies: A Report of a Conference on the State of the Field," *International Security* 12, no. 4 (Spring 1988), pp. 5–27; Helga Haftendorn, "The Security Puzzle: Theory-Building and Discipline-Building in International Security," *International Studies Quarterly* 35, no. 1 (March 1991), pp. 3–17.

8. For an analysis of domestic sources of the comparative advantage of industries in global markets see Michael E. Porter, *The Competitive Advantage of Nations* (New York: Free Press 1990).

9. Bruce Russett, "The Mysterious Case of Vanishing Hegemony; or, Is Mark Twain Really Dead?" *International Organization* 39, no. 2 (Spring 1985), pp. 228–230; Susan Strange, "The Persistent Myth of Lost Hegemony," *International Organization* 41, no. 4 (Autumn 1987), pp. 573–574.

10. Robert D. Putnam, "Diplomacy and Domestic Politics: The Logic of Two-Level Games," *International Organization* 41, no. 3 (Summer 1988), pp. 427–460.

PART ONE

Structures

2

Power, Polarity, and the Challenge of Disintegration

Stephen D. Krasner

For academics and the attentive public, two approaches dominate thinking about international affairs. The first, commonly labeled realism, emphasizes the anarchic character of the international system and the relative power of states. The second approach emphasizes the importance of domestic politics, seeing the basic motivation for foreign policy not in the anarchic nature of the international system or the eternal quest for power but rather in the domestic sociopolitical and economic characteristics of different states. Some domestic institutional arrangements are inherently peaceful; others are inherently aggressive.

This chapter self-consciously adopts a realist perspective. The starting point for any analysis of international politics must be the distribution of power. The behavior of individual states, regardless of their domestic political characteristics, is constrained by their own capabilities and the distribution of power in the system as a whole. States may, for some period of time, play too great a role or too small a role (given their power capabilities); such situations are inherently unstable. The external environment will inevitably pressure states to move toward congruity between commitments and capabilities. How graciously and effectively states respond to such pressure determines how stable the system will be.

In claiming that the international distribution of power is the starting point for understanding international politics, realism need not dismiss the importance of domestic politics. It need not claim that given the same distribution of power that democratic and authoritarian regimes would behave in exactly the same way; that the behavior of, say, the Federal Republic of Germany and the Third

Reich could be understood without reference to their domestic political characteristics. What realism does assert, however, is that the range of options available to any state is constrained by the international distribution of power. The most important fact about the United States as opposed to Albania is not the nature of their domestic political regimes but rather their respective power capabilities. Domestic politics matters, but only within constraints established by the distribution of power among states.

For realism the most salient facts about the contemporary international system are the following.

First, the power of the United States has declined. In the early postwar period the United States had a preponderance of capabilities across all power resources with the exception of ideological appeal, for which Marxist doctrines appeared to be a viable alternative, and military capabilities, for which the Soviet Union presented first a land-based and later a nuclear challenge. Although the resources of the United States remain formidable, especially with regard to military capability, America's relative strength in other areas, such as monetary reserves, trade, technology, and energy, has declined.

Second, the power of the Soviet Union, which had been overestimated in the past, is faltering in the present. Its military strength is still very significant, but its overall economic resources have declined relative to those of the West. The international appeal of its ideology has weakened if not evaporated.

Third, Japan and a unified Germany have been the great gainers with regard to power capability since the 1950s. Their potential power, as indicated by aggregate economic output, has grown substantially. Japan holds more international reserves than any other country. It has challenged the United States in many rapid-growth high-technology industries.

In sum, the world has been moving from a period of American hegemony in which the United States enjoyed a dominant, indeed domineering, position across a very wide range of issue areas, especially in the non-Communist world, to a period in which the distribution of power is, paradoxically, more unipolar but less hierarchical. The United States has lost power in relation to its allies but gained with respect to the Soviet Union. The distribution of power is, at the same time, both flatter and more single peaked.

The developments of the late 1980s are not equivalent to a great power war that fundamentally alters the distribution of power in the international system. Rather, recent changes have clarified a situation that was not adequately recognized—the weakness of the Soviet Union. The direct manifestation of this weakness has been the collapse of the Soviet Empire in Central Europe, a collapse that was contingent on the choices of a specific leader rather than an inevitable manifestation of a loss of power. Nevertheless, Gorbachev would never have been faced with such choices in the first place had the aggregate capabilities of the Soviet Union not deteriorated so dramatically compared with those of the West. Other basic attributes of the system have not changed. The prospects for peace among major states, assured by nuclear weapons, was high even during the Cold War, remains high today, and will continue to be high in the future regardless of domestic developments in the Soviet Union barring some technological breakthrough that would undermine assured second-strike capability.

The tensions and instabilities that exist in the present system are, aside from the uncertainty in Central Europe, more the result of longer-term trends in the international distribution of power—the decline of overweening American hegemony and the rise of Germany and especially, Japan. Power transitions are never easy. Declining states are reluctant to give up their past prerogatives and tend to be overcommitted. Rising states may be reluctant to assume responsibilities that only they can bear given their newly acquired capabilities. Specifically, the United States is still doing too much, and Japan and Germany (or perhaps Europe as a whole) are doing too little.

Realism suggests that through one path or another the United States will play a less ambitious role in the future. Both Europe and Japan will become more reluctant to follow the American lead. The United States will become less willing to bear a disproportionate share of the cost of maintaining stability in the system.

The rhetorical vision now articulated by most major Western leaders—the continuation of a strong NATO led by the United States and the development of a stronger European Community capable of formulating integrated security and foreign policies—is untenable. If the European Community becomes a truly integrated entity, there would be no need for a strong American-dominated Atlantic Alliance. Even if the European Community becomes nothing more than a single market, a continued major American presence in Europe would be difficult to legitimate to either European or American electorates even if, under conditions such as the disintegration of the Soviet Union and collapse in Central Europe, it would be justified by realist precepts.

With a flatter international hierarchy of power, American policies will become more self-interested, that is, more focused on specific shorter-term interests and less concerned with long-term regime stability. America as a more normal power will be neither imperial nor isolationist. In sum, its policies will be more like those of other states.

THE COLD WAR WORLD: BEGINNINGS

The most striking fact about the Cold War period was the preponderance of power enjoyed by the United States. The American economy was the only major industrial center that avoided the devastation of war. After World War II, the gross national product (GNP) of the United States was about three times larger than that of the Soviet Union and six times larger than that of Great Britain, its nearest non-Communist rival. Not only was the United States large in terms of aggregate economic output, it also enjoyed a dominant position in a very wide range of issue areas. It was the only state at the end of the war to possess nuclear weapons. Although its army had been demobilized, it maintained a formidable blue water navy and, as the Korean War demonstrated, could mobilize a large land force for combat thousands of miles from its shores. It was the center of technological development. Its companies dominated advanced industrial sectors. It had not only a surplus of food production but also a surplus of energy production. Until 1970 the United States was a net exporter of petroleum.

This extraordinary range of power assets was reflected in the extraordinarily ambitious policies pursued by the United States. The United States permanently garrisoned a large land army in Western Europe, especially Germany, and in Japan. It maintained naval bases around the world. It offered a nuclear guarantee to Western Europe and Japan with no direct military quid pro quo. In the economic arena, the United States was the moving force behind the creation of the Bretton Woods institutions, the World Bank, and the International Monetary Fund (IMF), the principal proponent of the General Agreement on Tariffs and Trade (GATT) (although the proposed International Trade Organization failed because of opposition in the American Congress), the largest source of foreign aid, and a supporter of European unity and Japanese and European reconstruction.

When American commitments to its allies were first made, they were consistent with both domestic sentiments in the United States and Europe and the distribution of power in the international system. Twice in the twentieth century the United States had chosen to intervene in European wars even though the territorial and political integrity of the United States was not directly threatened.

American intervention occurred only because its enormous power resources made it possible to pursue milieu goals: promoting an international environment that was consistent with American domestic values. After World War II, historical experience provided an incentive to maintain an ongoing commitment in Europe once American leaders were convinced of the hostile intent of the Soviet Union, which espoused a doctrine that was both universalistic (and therefore immanently expansionist) and profoundly alien to American liberalism's commitment to democracy and capitalism.

Europe's postwar democracies welcomed American military support. For Great Britain the Atlantic Alliance represented a deepening of the special relationship and an orientation that would allow Britain to continue to maneuver between the United States and the continent. France welcomed a continuation of the wartime alliance, although French leaders, especially Charles de Gaulle, were leery of American dominance and reliability. For West Germany, integration into a larger military alliance was the only strategic option; unilateralism was not attractive within Germany, nor would it have been acceptable to the other countries of Western Europe or the United States. Even divided, Germany was still a formidable power, and the memory of World Wars I and II could not simply be erased.[1]

The alliance system was congruent with the distribution of power, not just with specific national policy preferences. World War II had weakened, truncated, and divided Germany, creating a very different situation than the one that had existed in 1939 or 1914. Because of geographic proximity, and perhaps ideological differences as well, the Soviet Union, not the United States, was the major threat to Western Europe.

The countries of Western Europe, however, needed a powerful external ally. Their economies were still in disarray. The British failed to develop nuclear weapons during World War II and did not explode their first atomic bomb until 1952.[2] Although the United States was deficient in terms of conventional ground forces in comparison with the Soviet Union, it possessed a preponderance of nuclear weapons and associated delivery systems during the first two decades of the alliance. As long as the Soviets lacked the ability to launch a major nuclear strike against the United States, extended deterrence remained highly credible. The structural condition of the postwar world made the United States a very attractive partner.

The basic objective of American foreign economic policy in the early postwar years was to build up the economies of its allies. The lesson of the 1930s was that economic weakness could lead to political instability, and political instability to authoritarian regimes.

The United States wanted an economically strong Western Europe because it wanted to spread democracy and capitalism, to halt the expansion of communism, and to balance against the Soviet Union. Such ambitious policies were only possible because of the overwhelming power of the United States.

By the winter of 1946–1947 American policymakers had concluded that the wartime alliance with the Soviet Union had collapsed. They responded with a massive effort to use economic resources to inoculate Western Europe, Japan, and ultimately the Third World against Leninist regimes and Soviet enticements.[3]

The Marshall Plan provided large amounts of capital and foreign exchange that was designed to encourage productive investment in Europe and to facilitate European cooperation. The United States did not oppose the imposition of tariffs and quotas by European states. It supported the creation of the European Common Market even though a common external tariff would inevitably have some trade-diverting impact on the United States. After the unsuccessful effort to establish convertibility for the British pound in 1946, Europeans were allowed, even encouraged, to continue monetary policies that discriminated against the American dollar. Many European currencies were massively devalued in 1949. Although these devaluations were initiated by Europeans, they were supported by the United States. The European Payments Union, partially funded by the United States, facilitated trade.[4]

In sum, the policies followed by the United States through the mid-1960s were consistent with its overweening power and welcomed by its allies, who feared the Soviet Union and appreciated access to American markets and capital.

CHANGING CAPABILITIES

Over time the power of the United States deteriorated—hardly a surprising development given that Europe and Japan were bound to recover from the devastation of World War II.[5] With aggregate economic output used as an indicator of overall aggregate power, the relative position of the United States declined from the late 1940s until about 1970 and has remained more or less stable since then. The U.S. share of total OECD (Organization for Economic Cooperation and Development) production fell from 58 percent in 1953 to 38 percent in 1975. Since that time it has remained relatively constant, accounting for 35 percent of output in 1988.

With regard to individual countries, the most dramatic decrease in relative position has occurred in relationship to Japan. American output was more than ten times greater than that of Japan in 1960; by the late 1980s it was only about 70 percent greater. The next largest market economy, Germany, is only about one quarter the size of the United States. The Soviet Union grew faster than the United States in the 1950s and 1960s, but it has fallen further and further behind since the 1970s. Its overall output is probably now less than half that of the United States.[6]

Per capita output is a rough indicator of technological capability and factor mobility, considerations that determine whether a state can redeploy its resources to resist a foreign threat or to increase its leverage. As with aggregate production, the per capita output of the United States vis-à-vis other industrializing countries declines until the 1970s and then levels off with the exception of Japan.

The American share of world trade has followed a pattern similar to that of aggregate output, falling in the immediate postwar period and remaining steady at between 24 and 28 percent of total world trade (exports plus imports) over the past two decades. The division between exports and imports has, however, changed dramatically with the United States, moving from a large net exporter in the earlier postwar period to a large net importer during the 1980s. Although the United States continues to account for a larger share of world imports than any other country, it has sometimes fallen behind Germany in share of world exports.[7]

As Albert Hirschman so elegantly demonstrated in *National Power and the Structure of Foreign Trade*,[8] the basic relationship between trade and power is determined by the relative opportunity cost of change. The larger, more diverse, and more flexible an economy, the easier it is to adjust. The smaller, more concentrated, and more rigid an economy, the more difficult it is to adjust. Hence a large, diverse, and developed country like the United States is less subject to external economic pressures than other states and more able to make credible threats because the cost of implementing these threats is relatively low. If relative opportunity costs of change are used as a measure of power capabilities, then the position of the United States remains formidable.

One area where American capabilities have unambiguously declined is monetary reserves. The U.S. share of world monetary reserves fell from 50 percent in 1948 to 15 percent in 1970, remained at 13 to 17 percent during the mid-1980s, and then fell to under 10 percent in 1988. Japan passed the United States as the country with the largest international reserves in 1987, the first time that the United States had not ranked first in the postwar period.

Low reserves have not constrained the United States as severely as they would other countries. The United States is able to create money that foreigners are willing to hold because of the dollar's position as the world's primary reserve and transactions currency. And the United States is the only country that is able to borrow substantial amounts from foreigners in its own currency. The American position is, however, not as comfortable as it was before 1970, when the dollar was essentially the world's only transactions and reserve currency and the United States held much larger reserves than anyone else. Although the United States is probably still the world's most secure large parking space for capital, it is not the only garage in town. American central bankers have been constrained by the need to attract foreign capital to finance the U.S. budget deficit. The loss of reserves has meant that American policymakers are more sensitive to the external environment, less able to finance their way out of problems, and more impelled to consider other more substantial changes such as import controls, devaluation, or macroeconomic adjustment. As a major debtor rather than creditor, the United States has been less able to influence the policies of borrowers even though it is still able to hold its lenders hostage.[9]

There are other areas where the power capabilities of the United States have declined. The United States no longer has, as it did before 1970, surplus crude oil production capacity that could be used to offset cutbacks by Third World oil-exporting states. After the 1967 war in the Middle East, some oil-exporting states did attempt to impose production cutbacks. They were, however, frustrated by increases in exports from the Western Hemisphere, including the United States.

In contrast, the dramatic oil price increases of 1973–1974 and 1979–1980 had sharply negative consequences for the world economy. The United States went from being a net oil exporter to a net oil importer in 1970; it could no longer offset reductions in production elsewhere. Moreover, by the early 1970s the seven major oil companies (five of which were American) had made considerable concessions to host country governments. The companies could no longer dictate production levels. The price increases of 1973–1974 ushered in a period of lower productivity growth throughout the world because of the need to adjust to higher energy costs. Spiraling energy charges also contributed to higher rates of inflation. The price increases associated with the Iraqi occupation of Kuwait in 1990 and 1991 were less steep and less enduring, but even they reinforced recessionary trends in the United States.

The international oil market, like international financial markets, touches all countries. Energy is a sufficiently important sector of the economy that price changes in this one commodity can have significant consequences. It was not just to oppose what President Bush so often termed "naked aggression" that the United States dispatched over 400,000 troops to the Arabian peninsula.

In sum, American power has declined since the end of World War II. This is hardly surprising. Western Europe and Japan were destined to recover from the devastation of the war, even if it was difficult to predict that they would recover so well. This decline in relative American capability was most pronounced before 1970. Some major indicators of capabilities, especially share of world gross national product, have remained fairly stable since then. The United States still remains by far the world's largest and most diverse economy.

Nevertheless, the recovery of Europe and Japan and other shifts in capabilities have eroded the relative position of the United States. The United States has moved from being a net creditor to a major net debtor, making American financial markets sensitive to external developments and constraining the freedom of action of U.S. policymakers. Japan has challenged the preeminence of the United States in many high-technology industries. The Soviets have long since achieved nuclear parity. Most pointedly, the United States lost control of the world oil market shortly after 1970 when it moved from being a net oil exporter to a net importer and was, therefore, not able to offset production cutbacks imposed by Middle East producers after the 1973 war—cutbacks that had a devastating immediate effect on growth and inflation in the rest of the world and a long-term effect on growth and Third World debt. The inability of the United States to effectively regulate world oil markets led to the 1991 Gulf War, the first armed conflict over raw materials supplies since Japan attacked Pearl Harbor and British colonies in Asia in 1941.

CHANGING AMERICAN POLICY

Consistent with realist analysis, the decline in American power has been accompanied by changes in American policy in both the economic and the security areas. These changes, however, have come in fits and starts and have not been accompanied by any new strategic vision.

Defense expenditures offer one example of changing relative commitments. A decline in the power of the United States, operationalized here in terms of aggregate economic output, ought to, from a realist perspective, lead to a reduction in relative defense outlays. This has not been the case.

America's share of OECD aggregate output fell from the late 1940s until 1970. This change in underlying economic and strategic capabilities did not, however, result in a corresponding shift in military burdens to U.S. allies. The American share of NATO expenditures declined from 67 percent in 1955 to 62 percent in 1965 to 56 percent in 1975. This pattern corresponds very nicely with the predictions of realist theory: A relative decline in underlying resources led to a decrease in the share of military costs. The relationship between underlying resources and military burden, however, was reversed during the late Carter and especially the Reagan years. By 1985, America's share of NATO expenses had increased to 62 percent, the same level as in 1965. In the early 1980s European defense expenditures rose about 1.45 percent per annum, whereas those of the United States increased by 6.25 percent.[10]

The increase in American expenditures was driven by perceptions of Soviet behavior. It was, however, the United States and not the rest of NATO that acted to offset the Soviet Union, despite explicit commitments by European states to increase their defense budgets by 3 percent per annum.[11]

The Pentagon budget is now scheduled to be cut by 20 percent over the next several years. This would bring American expenditures more closely into line with its declining aggregate resource base.

In contrast with relative expenditures, American strategic doctrine did change in response to changing external conditions—more specifically, the Soviet development of strategic nuclear weapons capability. The doctrine of massive retaliation could, with some plausibility, be linked with extended deterrence so long as the Soviet Union could not threaten the United States. The notion, however, that the United States would launch a massive attack against the USSR in response to a Soviet attack on Western Europe was much less credible once the Soviets were in a position to destroy the United States. Well before the Soviets achieved nuclear parity, American planners were developing a new doctrine, that of flexible response, which was designed to raise the credibility of the American guarantee to Europe by giving U.S. policymakers more options.

John F. Kennedy's secretary of defense, Robert McNamara, was particularly interested in providing NATO with the conventional capability to resist a Soviet attack, placing the onus for any escalation to the nuclear level on the aggressor. In 1967, NATO formally accepted the principle of direct defense, which posited that the alliance should be able to respond to aggression at any level. The strategic doctrine of the United States changed from massive retaliation to flexible response as a result of the increase in Soviet capabilities, although the commitment to defend Western Europe with American troops and American nuclear weapons did not waiver from the 1950s through the 1980s.[12]

The fact that the United States was committed to Europe did not, however, mean that Europe would simply endorse American policy in other areas. U.S. leverage has decreased over time along with its relative capabilities. Even in the 1950s, at the apex of U.S. power, American policymakers were not able to secure French acceptance of the proposed European Defense Community. France formally withdrew from NATO in 1966.

During the early postwar years, however, the United States did generally get what it wanted. Several European states committed troops in the Korean War. Britain and France were forced to withdraw from Suez in 1956. The United States was able to impose its very conservative view of trade with the Soviet bloc onto its European allies.[13]

Policy coordination has become more difficult for the United States over time. Europe provided little backing for the American effort in Vietnam. The American attempt to prevent European exports to build the Siberian pipeline failed miserably. Only Britain supported the 1986 bombing of Libya.

As the underlying power capabilities of the United States and Europe have become more symmetrical, American leverage has declined. This is hardly cataclysmic; it is, in fact, a more normal state of affairs. What was abnormal was the a priori presumption of cooperation that masked the fact that European compliance with American preferences often reflected the preponderance of American power, not an underlying identity of interests.

The naval operations in the Persian Gulf during the Iran-Iraq war, which involved warships from both the United States and Europe, demonstrated that military cooperation is possible in third areas, although even in this instance the commitments of the United States were disproportionate to its direct economic interests. The effort to thwart Iraq's takeover of Kuwait demonstrated the continued military dominance of the United States with particular vengeance. American troops far outstripped those of any other country. France, and especially Britain, provided substantial forces, but Germany did not.

If the importance of Middle East oil is indicated by how much of a country's energy is supplied from that area, there is an inverse relationship between military commitments in the Gulf, with the two most energy-independent Western countries, the United States and Britain, sending the largest contingent of forces, and the most energy-dependent states, most notably Japan, sending none at all. Something is wrong here.

Prescriptively, the United States is still doing more than would be expected on the basis of its underlying power capabilities. Analytically, the disproportionate share of American military force in the Gulf can be explained by the logic of collective action: The United States provides a disproportionate share of collective defense because of its size; it makes sense for smaller countries to free ride.

The pattern of American foreign economic policy more closely follows realist predictions, although here, too, there are anomalies. In practice, the United States has moved away from a focus on milieu goals toward greater concern with specific American economic objectives, whereas rhetorically American leaders have continued to defend a liberal, open international economic order. The Reagan administration venerated the free market. The United States took the lead in the possibly defunct Uruguay Round of multilateral trade negotiations that was designed to extend the scope of GATT coverage to services as well as deal with a number of enduring issues including agricultural subsidies.

Although the general principles and commitments of American policymakers have not changed, both external and internal pressures have led to the adoption of new policies that are based more on specific than diffuse reciprocity.[14] American foreign economic policy has not been characterized by the replacement of one set of principles by another but rather by the accretion of one set of practices on top of other earlier practices that might have been based on different principles and norms.[15] Even in the 1950s U.S. policymakers employed sector-specific approaches. The motivation of executive branch officials was to preempt what they feared would be even more restrictive action initiated by Congress. They frequently resorted to voluntary export restraints (VERs) as the least damaging form of protectionism. "Voluntary" restraints did not formally violate GATT rules. VERs gave the rents accruing from restricted access to foreign producers rather than to the U.S. Treasury, an indication that the primary concern of American leaders was to preserve, as best as they could in face of domestic protectionist pressures, an open global system rather than to maximize returns to the United States.

Trade legislation since 1970 has been more concerned with specific American interests than the stability of the global economic system as a whole. The Trade Act of 1974 mandated that Congress, which was generally more protectionist than the executive, had to approve any trade agreement by a majority vote of both houses. The requirements for invoking provisions of the escape clause were relaxed, making it easier for American industries that were harmed by imports to get relief. Perhaps most important, the 1974 act introduced a broad notion of unfair trading practices under section 301 of the act. The Trade Act of 1979 moved jurisdiction over the three elements of American law that dealt with what were considered unfair foreign practices—dumping, subsidies, and 301 violations—from the jurisdiction of the Treasury Department, which had been strongly committed to free trade, over to the Commerce Department, which was more responsive to the interests of particular American industries.

The Trade and Tariff Act of 1984 gave the president the right to negotiate bilateral free trade agreements, a movement away from generalized most favored nation treatment. Agreements have been concluded with Israel and, much more significant, with Canada. The United States and Mexico are actively exploring a free trade agreement, raising the promise or specter of a North American trading bloc.

The Omnibus Trade and Competitiveness Act of 1988 created a number of mechanisms that could, if they were vigorously pursued by the executive branch, provide the United States with greater leverage to alter the behavior of foreign trading partners. Most important, the Super 301 provision of the act provides for expedited action against countries that are judged to be engaged in unfair trading practices. Such practices can, under the provisions of this act, be technically legal, but if they violate the spirit of international trade agreements the president is authorized to retaliate. Retaliation can be targeted against a specific country and can take a very wide range of forms. Super 301 is an instrument for coercive bargaining on the part of the United States. It has been used as leverage to get other countries to change their policies.[16]

The growing American concern with specific interests has not been limited to the area of trade and investment. In the 1980s, American officials pressed other countries to open their telecommunications markets to both American products and services. A more market-oriented regime would undermine the system of national monopolies that has dominated domestic and international markets since the nineteenth century. In fall 1990, however, American policymakers backed away from their demand for national treatment in fear that foreign competitors would secure more advantages in the open American market than American companies could secure in more restricted European markets.[17]

American international monetary policies since the early 1970s are best explained in terms of the concrete and specific interests of the United States. American leaders have moved away from policies of the 1960s, which were dominated by a concern for global stability. When the U.S. trade balance, as opposed to just the current account balance, fell into deficit in 1971, the Nixon administration acted decisively to bring down the value of the dollar by suspending gold convertibility and imposing an almost across-the-board 10 percent import surcharge. This unilaterally destroyed the Bretton Woods system. In the early 1980s the Reagan administration conducted macroeconomic policy exclusively through monetary rather than fiscal policy, forcing global interest rates up and greatly exacerbating the debt problems of Third World countries. American international monetary policy has been increasingly driven by specific interests rather than milieu goals.[18]

In sum, in both security and economic arenas American policies have moved away from milieu goals and have become more focused on specific American interests. At the same time, the rhetoric and the general principles espoused by American leaders have not changed. The United States continues to support NATO and its alliance with Japan. It has not backed away from extended deterrence; no American policymaker has indicated that the nuclear umbrella will be closed.

With regard to international economic policy, specific policies have increasingly diverged from the norms of diffuse reciprocity, openness, and nondiscrimination. Various pressures, sometimes from domestic groups, and sometimes from the international system, have compelled policymakers to adopt practices that are increasingly concerned with specific, well-defined American interests. Unlike the early Cold War years when power, rhetoric, and policy were internally consistent and reinforcing, the period since 1970 has been less coherent. Policies are inconsistent with espoused principles and norms because the relationship between underlying capabilities and commitments is more problematic. This pattern of behavior is at least generally consistent with the expectations of a realist perspective.

SPECULATIONS

If relative state power is the master variable for understanding international politics, what should the post–Cold War world look like?

Taking GNP as the simplest measure of aggregate power, consider what the distribution of capabilities might look like in the year 2000 or 2010. Table 2.1 simply extrapolates growth rates for the period

TABLE 2.1   Projected Gross National Product, 2000 and 2010 (in millions of dollars)

	1980–1987 Growth Rate (percent)	GNP		
		1987	*2000*	*2010*
United States	2.5	4,486,176	6,181,950	7,895,670
USSR	2.7	2,399,024	3,382,624	4,414,204
Japan	3.8	1,925,614	3,119,494	4,525,192
Germany	1.0	1,111,381[a]	1,266,974	1,400,340
France	1.2	714,994	922,342	1,129,691
United Kingdom	2.6	592,946	830,124	1,067,302
Italy	1.5	596,995	722,363	841,762

[a]Based on a unified Germany with East German GNP per capita equal to that of West Germany. West German GNP was $879 million.

SOURCES: World Bank, *World Bank Atlas* (Washington, D.C.: World Bank, 1988) for 1987 GNP and growth rates. USSR data derived from CIA, *Handbook of Economic Statistics* (Washington, D.C.: Government Printing Office, 1985).

1980–1987 into the future, beginning with aggregate GNP in 1987. The entry for Germany assumes that the former German Democratic Republic (GDR) will secure the same level of per capita GNP as the rest of the Federal Republic and that the growth rate for the new Germany can be extrapolated from that of what was West Germany.

Table 2.2 shows the percentage of GNP accounted for by each of these seven countries; that is, each individual GNP divided by the total GNP for the seven.

Different assumptions about growth rates do change predictions. To take an extreme, assume that the two largest states, the Soviet Union and the United States, grow at the slow rate of 1.0 percent per annum until the year 2010. Japan continues to grow at the 3.8 percent rate of the 1980s. Assume that all of the major countries of the Community—Germany, France, Italy, and Britain—grow at the relatively rapid rate of 2.6 percent per annum, the rate experienced by Britain during the 1980-1987 period. The percentage of GNP for the seven major countries would then be distributed as shown in Table 2.3.

It should be noted that this is not a very likely scenario; it would imply that per capita Japanese GNP was 60 percent greater than that of the United States, assuming that both countries had the same rate of population growth. In fact, the U.S. rate of population growth for the period 1980–1987 was 1.0 percent/annum and that of Japan was 0.6 percent/annum.[19]

Compared with 1987, the major consequence of these hypothetical growth rates is that the positions of Japan and the Soviet Union are reversed with Japan clearly emerging as the second-largest power.

TABLE 2.2   Projected Percentage Shares of Gross National Product, 2000 and 2010

	1987	2000	2010
United States	38	37	37
USSR	20	21	21
Japan	16	19	21
Germany	9	8	7
France	6	6	5
United Kingdom	5	5	5
Italy	5	4	4

SOURCES: World Bank, *World Bank Atlas* (Washington, D.C.: World Bank, 1988), for 1987 GNP data. USSR data derived from CIA, *Handbook of Economic Statistics* (Washington, D.C.: Government Printing Office, 1985).

TABLE 2.3   Projected Percentage Shares of Gross National Product, 2010, with Slow Growth for the United States and the USSR

United States	30
USSR	16
Japan	24
Germany	10
France	7
United Kingdom	6
Italy	6

These simple, even simple-minded, extrapolations raise questions about the easy assumption that the world is becoming multipolar. At a global level the United States continues to be the state with the most formidable power capabilities. Nevertheless, the erosion of American capacity in some specific issue areas (noted earlier) is likely to continue.

If the European Community is considered as a single entity, however, the picture changes radically. The European Community, taken as a whole, has somewhat greater power capabilities than the United States. A world in which Europe had an integrated foreign and security policy, not just an integrated internal market, would, at the very least, be bipolar. The United States could not be regarded as the single dominant power.

The distributions of underlying power capabilities displayed in Tables 2.2 and 2.3 suggest that the pattern of obligations assumed by the United States after World War II will change, especially if Europe becomes more politically united. The one configuration of policy that is not tenable in the long run is exactly the policy that is now being advocated by most European and American leaders—a strong NATO and a strong European Community into which Germany is tightly integrated. If the European Community does become an effective political and security entity, then the Atlantic Alliance understood as a regime based upon an American-led NATO, an American nuclear guarantee for Europe, and large numbers of American troops stationed in Germany is finished. Even before the Soviets abandoned Central Europe, American commitments were excessive. They were based upon power configurations that existed in the 1950s, even the late 1940s, when Western Europe had not recovered from the devastation of World War II and the Soviets could pose a credible military threat. It is difficult to see what rationale could be provided for the continuation of NATO as an American-dominated alliance in an environment composed of a united Europe with an aggregate GNP larger than that of the United States and a weakened Soviet Union. Europe could develop its own nuclear forces, which would provide a more credible deterrent against attack than any version of the extended deterrence that has been offered by the United States.

A continued American presence in Europe and a strong NATO led by the United States would make sense only if the European Community were weak, that is, if the Community failed to develop an integrated security and foreign policy. The purpose of American forces would then be to balance not only against the Soviet Union, or what is left of it, but also against Germany. From a realist perspective 1990 does, in some ways, look like 1914 or 1939. Germany is again the most powerful state in the center of Europe and could again become a threat to, and be threatened by, its neighbors. In such a multipolar environment misperception and miscalculation are endemic problems; the failure of other states to balance against Germany did contribute to the outbreak of war in 1914 and 1939. Europe could encourage the continued involvement of the United States as a counterbalance to Germany.[20]

It is, however, unlikely that the United States will play such a role or that Europe would welcome it. There is, in the first place, one critical difference between 1914 or 1939 and 1990—the existence of nuclear weapons. The traditional European balance of power was based on force, but a consciously initiated major war in Europe is unthinkable, not because Germany is now a democracy but because nuclear weapons are so unambiguously destructive. Even very powerful conventional weapons held out the chance of decisive victory with limited losses, a possibility realized by Germany in 1940 and the United States in 1991. There can be no such hope in a nuclear war.

The negative side of nuclear weapons—the reason nuclear proliferation inspires such disquiet—is that things can always go wrong

not through intentional action but rather through organizational
failure or the actions of a madman. The more states there are with
nuclear weapons, the greater the risk, small though it may be. Hence
there must be some balancing between the stability provided by
nuclear proliferation and the dangers posed by the greater chance
(albeit still a very small chance) of inadvertent use. Even in the
context of a weak European Community, the procurement of some
form of limited nuclear capability by Germany would be highly
stabilizing and would undermine the rationale for continued
American commitment.

The main instruments of power and leverage in Europe in the
future will be economic rather than military. If the European
Community develops into an entity capable of formulating and
implementing unified security and foreign policies, an entity that
precludes an independent German foreign policy, then the vision of
Mitteleuropa, the center of Europe dominated by Germany, would
be irrelevant. If, however, such a pan-European entity does not
develop, then issues of German domination generated by power
asymmetries in the center of the continent could reassert themselves.
Under such conditions, the involvement of the United States as a
balancer might be attractive for Germany as well as the smaller
states of Central Europe.

Germany was the major economic partner for the states of Central
Europe before the creation of the Soviet bloc. Germany exported
sophisticated consumer and capital goods in exchange for agricultural
products, raw materials, and cheap manufactures. This pattern of
trade held for 100 years. Before World War I, Germany accounted
for 45 percent of Russian imports and 30 percent of Russian exports.
For Germany the totals were 8 percent of exports to Russia and 14
percent of imports from Russia. Russia needed the German market
for its grain much more than Germany needed the Russian market
for its manufactures.

In 1929 Germany accounted for 30 percent of Polish trade but
Poland accounted for only 3 percent of German trade. Germany
absorbed 28 percent of Czech exports and supplied 40 percent of
Czech imports. The Soviet Union was relatively isolated, but the
German share of Soviet imports was 28 percent in 1928 and the
Soviets accounted for 3 percent of German sales.[21] The creation of
the Communist bloc radically altered these trading patterns. The
economies of Central Europe were organized along the Soviet
Stalinist model, which emphasized heavy industry, central planning,
and self-sufficiency.[22] The limited amount of trade generated in this
system was oriented toward the Soviet Union. In 1960, perhaps the
apex of the Cold War, 84 percent of Bulgarian trade (imports plus

exports) went to the Soviet area, 69 percent of Czechoslovakian trade, 70 percent of East German trade, 66 percent of Hungarian trade, 60 percent of Polish trade, and 71 percent of Romanian trade. Only 28 percent of Yugoslavian trade went to the Soviet area. In contrast, trade with the Federal Republic varied from 10 percent for the GDR, 7 percent for Romania, 5 percent for Poland and Hungary, 4 percent for Bulgaria, and 3 percent for Czechoslovakia.[23]

The economies of the smaller states of Eastern and Central Europe are changing quickly. It is not yet evident what the long-term trading pattern will be; more to the point, whether Germany either as an inextricable part of a more integrated European Community or as an independent state will again become the economic linchpin of Central Europe. Table 2.4 shows trade (exports plus imports) of Hungary, Poland, and Romania with Germany, the United States, the Soviet Union, and France, Britain, and Italy combined in 1989.

Trade with Germany is more important than trade with any other Western state, but the numbers are far from overwhelming. The Soviet Union still dominated trade with its former satellites in the late 1980s. The pattern for Yugoslavia, which had broken with the Soviet Union, is not so different. In 1988 the Soviet bloc accounted for 23 percent of Yugoslavian trade (of which the Soviet Union itself accounted for 16 percent), Germany 14 percent (16 percent if the former GDR is included), France, Britain, and Italy 19 percent, and the United States 6 percent.[24] None of these figures suggest that *Mitteleuropa* (the center of Europe dominated by German economic power) is inevitable. Only if the Soviet economy collapses or the Stalinist autarkic model is reimposed could trade concentrations between Germany and the smaller states of Eastern and Central Europe come to resemble the highly asymmetrical pattern that characterized the 1930s, a situation that would invite the use of economic coercion. Under such conditions a continued strong American political and even military presence in Europe might be welcomed, especially if the European Community were weak.

The looming problem in Central Europe is not the danger of German domination but the possibility of economic and political disintegration. At least some of the Central European states might not successfully traverse the distance between their old systems and new regimes based on capitalism and democracy. Old ethnic tensions could become even more exacerbated. Armed conflict could occur.[25]

Under such conditions, who might intervene to provide stability and order? A strong European Community, one that does not yet exist, would be one obvious candidate. In the short and medium term, Germany could not act alone. It does not have the military power to maintain order in Central Europe if domestic regimes fail. German domestic sentiment would

TABLE 2.4   East European Trade, 1989 (percentage of exports plus imports)

	Germany	France, United Kingdom, Italy	USSR	United States
Hungary	18	10	28	3
Poland	12	10	33	2
Romania	4	7	33	2

SOURCE: Derived from figures in IMF, *Direction of Trade, Yearbook 1990* (Washington, D.C.: IMF, 1990), country pages. Czechoslovakia and Bulgaria are not included because the data source does not provide figures on their trade with the Soviet bloc.

not support an ambitious foreign policy. (In a recent poll conducted for the *Süddeutsche Zeitung,* Switzerland was identified by more Germans than any other country as a potential model. About 40 percent name Switzerland, followed by Sweden, Japan, and Italy. Only 6 percent listed the United States.)[26]

The most attractive way to manage and contain this potential instability would be for the United States and the Soviet Union to play an active peacekeeping role in the region.[27] The Soviet Union, however, may have troubles enough of its own, and the willingness of the United States to intimately involve itself in European affairs in the absence of some overarching ideological as well as political and military threat is problematic.

In sum, the United States is bound in the future to play a less ambitious role in Europe both economically and militarily. If the European Community evolves further and develops the capacity to formulate foreign and security policies, then there would be no function for the United States as a security guarantor. The German problem would be solved, and Europe could deter any military attack.

Even if a stronger European Community does not develop, it is difficult to specify constraints and incentives that would prompt a continuation of America's present policy. Absent Soviet collapse, there is no threat of a *Mitteleuropa* that might encourage Germany as well as the states of Central Europe to support a continued high profile for the United States. If the Soviet Union does collapse and the European Community fails to develop beyond an integrated market, it would still be very difficult for the United States to provide stability in Central Europe by continuing to station a large number of U.S. forces in Germany. Could the *Bundestag* really be sold on the continuation of American troop convoys clogging the autobahns, military exercises churning up farmland, or fighter jets flying low over populated areas to balance against the danger of German domination of Central Europe? The concept of containing Germany with traffic jams at the Frankfurt *Dreieck* would be a very tough sell, even if it would be consistent with realist prescriptions.

A reduced role for the United States in Europe would be a return to a more normal pattern of international politics. International economic relations would be characterized more by specific deals than general principles. Europe would assume responsibility for its own defense, and Germany would play a more prominent political and military role. There would be less power in the world because it would be more difficult to orchestrate the dispersed resources of several countries than it was for the United States to ferociously pursue a set of milieu goals designed to promote democracy and capitalism and to frustrate communism.

None of this implies that the world is condemned to a period of disorder. That greatest instrument of destruction, nuclear weapons, is also the greatest instrument of peace, for nuclear weapons have eliminated any ambiguity about the cost of war. The increasing openness of the global economy over the past forty-five years has given many interests a stake in the continuation of the present system. The world's largest corporations are almost all multinational. The ratio of trade to aggregate economic activity is at historically high levels. More self-interested conduct especially by the United States does not mean that the system will collapse, even if economic conflicts multiply. Because of the unambiguous destructive capability of nuclear weapons and the opportunities to secure wealth through exchange rather than invasion, the long peace that has prevailed in the industrialized North, including Europe, is likely to prevail despite the erosion of American and Soviet power and the ultimate demise of the Atlantic Alliance.

NOTES

1. William Park, *Defending the West: A History of NATO* (Brighton: Wheatsheaf 1986), pp. 7–20.

2. David N. Schwartz, *NATO's Nuclear Dilemmas* (Washington, D.C.: Brookings Institution 1983), pp. 26–31.

3. Robert Packenham, *Liberal America and the Third World* (Princeton: Princeton University Press 1973).

4. Thomas L. Ilgen, *Autonomy and Interdependence: U.S.–Western European Monetary and Trade Relations* (Totowa, N.J.: Rowman and Allenheld 1985), p. 12; Michael Webb, "International Coordination of Macro-Economic Policies, 1945–1989," Ph.D. dissertation, Stanford University 1990.

5. A.F.K. Organski and Jacek Kugler, *The War Ledger* (Chicago: University of Chicago Press 1980).

6. CIA (Central Intelligence Agency), *Handbook of Economic Statistics* (Washington, D.C.: Government Printing Office 1985); Stephen D. Krasner, "National Power and Global Communications," *World Politics* (April 1991), p. 346; OECD (Organization for Economic Cooperation and Development), Department of Economics and Statistics, *National Accounts, Main Aggregates,*

Volume 1, 1960–1986 (Paris: OECD 1990), Table 13 and p. 145; UN, *Yearbook of National Accounts Statistics, 1965* (New York: UN 1966).

7. UN, *Yearbook of International Trade Statistics, 1960, 1970–1971, and 1984* (New York: UN 1966); *GATT, International Trade,* various years.

8. Albert Hirschman, *National Power and the Structure of Foreign Trade* (Berkeley: University of California Press 1945).

9. IMF, *International Financial Statistics Yearbooks, 1987 and 1989* (Washington, D.C.: IMF 1987, 1989); Susan Strange, "The Persistent Myth of Lost Hegemony," *International Organization* 41, no. 1986, pp. 568–569.

10. IISS (International Institute for Strategic Studies), *The Military Balance, 1987–1988* (London: IISS 1987), pp. 215–216; Peter H. Langer, *Transatlantic Discord and NATO's Crisis of Cohesion* (Washington, D.C.: Pergamon-Brassey's 1986), p. 49.

11. Langer, *Transatlantic Discord,* p. 51.

12. David N. Schwartz, "A Historical Perspective," in John D. Steinbruner and Leon V. Sigal, eds., *Alliance Security: NATO and the No-First-Use Question* (Washington, D.C.: Brookings Institution 1983), pp. 5–21.

13. Bruce Jentleson, "From Consensus to Conflict: The Domestic Politics of East-West Energy Trade Policy," *International Organization* 38, no. 4 (Autumn 1984), pp. 625–660.

14. Robert Keohane, "Reciprocity in International Relations," *International Organization* 40, no. 1 (1986), pp. 1–27.

15. Judith Goldstein, "Ideas, Interests, and American Trade Policy," unpublished manuscript (Stanford: Stanford University, 1990).

16. Goldstein, "Ideas, Interests," pp. 47–52.

17. Krasner, "National Power and Global Communications"; Peter Cowhey, "The International Telecommunications Regime: The Political Roots of International Regimes for High Technology," *International Organization* 44, no. 1990.

18. Joanne Gowa, *Closing the Gold Window: Domestic Politics and the End of Bretton Woods* (Ithaca: Cornell University Press 1983).

19. World Bank, *World Bank Atlas* (Washington, D.C.: World Bank 1988), pp. 7, 9.

20. Ronald Steel, "Europe After the Superpowers," in Nicholas X. Rizopoulos, ed., *Sea-Changes: American Foreign Policy in a World Transformed* (New York: Council on Foreign Relations 1990), p. 18.

21. Robert Mark Spaulding, Jr., "German Trade Policy in Eastern Europe, 1890–1990," *International Organization* 45, no. 3 (Summer 1991), pp. 343–368.

22. Nina Halpern, "The Diffusion of Stalinist Political Economy," paper prepared for SSRC Conference on Ideas and Foreign Policy, Stanford University, April 29–30, 1991.

23. Derived from figures in IMF, *Direction of Trade Statistics, Yearbooks 1958–1962* (Washington, D.C.: IMF various years), country pages.

24. IMF, *Direction of Trade Statistics, Yearbook 1989* (Washington, D.C.: IMF 1989), pp. 417–418.

25. John Mearsheimer, "Back to the Future: Instability in Europe After the Cold War," *International Security* 15, no. 2 (1990).

26. *Financial Times,* January 4, 1991, p. 2.

27. Steel, "Europe After the Superpowers," pp. 17–18.

3

The Diplomacy of Structural Change:
Multilateral Institutions and
State Strategies

Robert O. Keohane

When the world is changing with dazzling speed, as it has been since 1989, professional students of international politics have the opportunity, and the obligation, to seek to use their theories to understand contemporary events. Indeed, to help us understand the world in which we live is the chief function of international theory. I will seek therefore to interpret some elements of change in contemporary world politics—taking the risk that events will soon prove me wrong! I am conscious that when we offer contemporary analysis and policy advice we must be humble: During the past several years we have failed to anticipate major changes in world politics much less to evaluate how particular policy actions affected events. Our conclusions about the present and our speculations about the future must be even more tentative than our judgments about the past.

The victory of the United States and its allies in the war against Iraq led to a spate of popular commentary in the United States about a "new world order" under the aegis of American military hegemony. Fortunately, some of the nonsense that appeared in the wake of the war has now dissipated. The Kurdish crisis, Iraqi attempts to hide their nuclear weapons research capabilities, and now the civil war in Yugoslavia have perhaps made even the most assertive

This chapter is based on a longer paper prepared for a volume tentatively entitled *Diplomacy, Force and Leadership: Essays in Honor of Alexander L. George,* edited by Dan Caldwell and Timothy J. McKeown.

Americans reflect on the intractability of the world and the limitations of American power. We are seeing both the resilience of authoritarian rule in Iraq and what John Mearsheimer has called "hypernationalism" in Europe. Freedom, Americans will learn once again, does not only have a benign face. It includes freedom to establish petty tyrannies, or to oppress other peoples—whether in Georgia, Yugoslavia, or Iraq. I recall the description given by Thucydides in *The Peloponnesian War* of the effects of revolution in Corcyra:

> Reckless audacity came to be considered the courage of a loyal ally; prudent hesitation, specious cowardice; moderation was held to be a cloak for unmanliness; ability to see all sides of the question, ineptness to act on any. Frantic violence became the attribute of manliness; cautious plotting, a justifiable means of self-defense. The advocate of extreme measures was always trustworthy; his opponent, a man to be suspected. [III, 82]

The "new world order" looks dubious now. Voltaire said of the Holy Roman Empire that it was neither holy, nor Roman, nor an empire. The "new world order" may be neither new, nor worldwide, nor an order.

Admittedly, the American feats of arms in the Gulf were impressive; they certainly showed that large but technologically backward conventional armies are much less severe threats against an advanced fighting force than had previously been believed. They should not, however, be interpreted as meaning that military force can achieve political change or maintain the rule of unpopular governments within countries—which the United States attempted in Vietnam and which the Serbian generals have been seeking in Yugoslavia. The defeat of conventional aggression can be achieved through massive air power, helicopter gunships, smart bombs, and air-land battle doctrines; governance is an entirely different matter. The United States could force Iraq from Kuwait, and it could at least temporarily protect the Kurds against Saddam's brutality, but it cannot install a decent government in Baghdad—or even in Kuwait City. Nor could Secretary James Baker persuade the Yugoslav leaders to negotiate seriously with one another.

It would also be simplistic to assume that the military victory of the United States in the Persian Gulf implies that the United States is once again "number one"—"hegemonic," in the term used by political scientists. Power depends on more than military strength. It depends at least as much on economic strength, the attractiveness of one's ideas and economic system, and one's willingness to spend resources on foreign policy. For many purposes—securing cooperation from other advanced societies, ensuring growth in the world economy, cleaning the global environment—military strength is not very important at all. It serves better as a shield against domination by others than as a positive means of influence.

Here I will try to put recent events in a broader historical and theoretical perspective and to draw some conclusions for policy. First, I will argue that if we view power more broadly than sheer military force, the past thirty years have witnessed a concentration of effective power resources in the capitalist world as a whole. That is, there has been a transformation of political structure. But within the capitalist world, power has become more complex and difficult to exercise and there has been a diffusion of effective power resources among capitalist states. Thus the new world is not "unipolar" in a meaningful sense, and a "new world order" will remain out of America's grasp. Only through the effective use of international institutions could some approximation to such an order be attained. In my view, U.S. policy needs to use international institutions to achieve any policy departures if not anything so grand as a "new world order."

THE TRANSFORMATION
OF POLITICAL STRUCTURE

What distinguishes the present period from previous periods of détente, as in the early 1970s, is the revelation of Soviet economic, political, and military weakness, the withdrawal of Soviet power from Eastern and Central Europe, and the reunification of Germany. If the Soviet Union (or at least Russia, linked to the Ukraine and Belorussia) manages to maintain its political integrity and remain a great power, conflicts of interest with Europe and the United States will persist. Depending on domestic politics, leadership policies, and events elsewhere, these conflicts may be more or less severe. However, they will be fundamentally different from the conflicts of the Cold War era because the Soviet Union will face a strong, reunited Germany with Poland between them. The Cold War began over the division of Germany and the Soviet takeover of Eastern Europe; the reversal of these actions marks its end.

Not only has the Soviet Union withdrawn from Eastern Europe; its status as a great power is in jeopardy for both economic and political reasons. Its capability to produce technologically sophisticated commercial products continues to fall further behind the capitalist world, its industrial production seems to be declining, and the performance of its distribution system has worsened markedly since 1989. At the same time, its political coherence is threatened both "horizontally" by regional conflicts among and within the various republics and "vertically" by political conflicts between traditional organs of the Soviet state and newly organized political forces. The Soviet Union faces the danger of economic collapse and civil war. This transformation is stunning, but because we are all aware of it I will not dwell on it.

If the Soviet empire had collapsed in 1953 and Germany had been reunited then, the world would have become unipolar, with the United States the sole superpower. It would, however, be very misleading to characterize the world of the 1990s in this way. Of course, the United States is the only state with the capacity to exercise global political leadership, as Joseph Nye has argued.[1] Thus in the short term, the United States is the only entity capable of coherent leadership outside of a circumscribed region. As Nye has argued, the United States is an expert in "power conversion"—defining purposes and bringing resources to bear on objectives. Japan is too hesitant and internally divided, Europe is too split among countries with very different orientations toward leadership to rival the United States. Furthermore, everyone expects the United States to exert leadership, which perpetuates American influence. Perhaps this is the most important aspect of "soft power."

But in the long term, U.S. leadership is not so well assured. In the past, sustained economic capabilities have almost always been converted into political leadership, although often with a lag. Japan is undoubtedly investing more than the United States, capturing more markets, growing faster, and closing the technological gap. Europe is becoming more united. Its market is already as large as that of the United States and is in the process of expanding to a European Economic Area of nineteen states with 380 million people. Furthermore, although the budgetary measures of October 1991 made some difference, the United States continues to run current account deficits, borrowing abroad. This pattern is inconsistent with long-run power; it will constrict American financial resources for dealing with a myriad of problems from the USSR to Latin America.

Focusing on the long term means that we need to think about the diffusion of power in the world capitalist system, which I believe to be a long-term trend. The diffusion of power has two major dimensions: (1) the expansion and globalization of interdependence and (2) the decline in the economic preponderance of the United States.

THE EXPANSION AND GLOBALIZATION
OF INTERDEPENDENCE

The first dimension of the diffusion of power concerns its increasing complexity. One dimension of this complexity involves the ambiguity of the concept of security, whether national or international. These ambiguities have been explored in a subtle and original way by Barry Buzan, who links security to the concept of interdependence and asks the often unspoken question "To whom does the phrase "security," when it is used, refer?[2] Deterrence is difficult; forcing others to act in desired ways through military threats is even harder. And if it is difficult to use threats of force even on military issues, it is often impossible to translate military force into political influence on most of the issues dividing the countries of the tripolar world economy. Nothing that happened in winter 1990 has altered the correctness of this judgment. It was always clear that if unchecked, aggressive states could seize their neighbors' territory. In that sense, military force is not obsolete and probably will never become so. But the limited utility of military force should not lead us to conclude that it is useful on all or most major issues. Threats or promises concerning force are very difficult to use on issues of trade barriers, macroeconomic policy coordination, or environmental protection. Movements of aircraft carriers will not open markets, alter exchange rates, or preserve tropical rain forests from destruction.

Nonmilitary issues have become more important during the past forty years, as interdependence has grown. Interdependence means that societies, firms, groups, and governments are both sensitive to actions of others and vulnerable to changes in their relationships induced by others' behavior. During the Cold War, trade consistently grew at a rate greater than that of world output. Between 1960 and 1986, foreign direct investment by developed market economies grew even more rapidly. Shifts in energy consumption and production increased the dependence of Europe, Japan, and the United States on oil from the Middle East. Reliance on air transport increased sensitivity to terrorism against commercial aircraft; the increased concern about environmental issues raised perceived interdependence about threats to the ozone layer, about global warming, and about transboundary pollution. Influence on these global issues depends very little on military power and a great deal on specific patterns of capability pertaining to issue areas. Oil exports, size of import market, possession of rain forests, or length and location of coastline (in the Law of the Sea debates) may all be power resources in some situations, such as determining oil prices, negotiating over trade barriers, deciding on global climate regimes, or bargaining over the Law of the Sea. But it is hard to exchange these resources for one another. They are not like money. A long coastline won't buy you cheaper oil; having a big import market could indirectly confer influence over a climate change regime, but the diplomacy involved would be tricky indeed.

Interdependence means that even great powers cannot act effectively on their own. To regain some influence over events, governments and firms have to collaborate with one another; they have to sacrifice their unilateral freedom of action for some degree of mastery over transnational flows of goods, capital, technology, ideas, and people. But because sovereignty remains the basis of world society, the sources of effective control over relevant state policy remain fragmented. As issues subject to interdependence proliferate, these power sources become more diffuse. Not only do they lie in the hands of more states, but within states they are controlled by more different types of actors.

Thus the general pattern during the past forty years has been one of great difficulty in using force except for deterrence, which is tricky enough, and of diffusion of power as the number of issues about which states negotiate has proliferated. During the Cold War, however, this diffusion of power was somewhat restrained by the fact that military force was a source of political influence for the United States in one very important respect. Because Europe and Japan relied on the American nuclear umbrella and substantial numbers of American troops for their security (or at least their confidence in their own security) against the Soviet Union, they had to worry that the United States might, either deliberately or as a result of popular pressure, reduce its protection for them if conflicts on other issues became too intense. Insofar as the Soviet Union becomes less of a threat, this source of U.S. influence may actually decline in the coming "new world order."

THE DECLINE OF AMERICAN
ECONOMIC PREPONDERANCE

Throughout the 1980s, political scientists argued about the changing configuration of world power. How concentrated are power resources and, in particular, how dominant is the United States? Is the American share of relevant power resources declining? If so, at what rate? What is the relationship between tangible power resources and actual influence in world politics?[3]

In my view, this debate has been somewhat overdramatized. The United States is no longer as dominant as it was thirty or forty years ago, and relative to East Asia it continues to lose ground in high technology as well as in manufacturing capability. But it is still the world's leading economic power and its decline has not been precipitous. Four points need to be made.

First, even during the height of its economic ascendance in the 1950s and into the early 1960s, the United States was involved in a bipolar military competition with the Soviet Union and was excluded by Soviet military power and political decisions from significant access to Eastern Europe and much of continental Asia. U.S. dominance was never global in scope; on the contrary, its impact was only strongly felt within the capitalist world economy.

Second, political scientists have sometimes exaggerated the ability of the United States to exert effective influence over its allies even when its material capacities were enormous. The United States did indeed seek to determine the strategic direction of Western policy and to induce its European partners, through provision of material benefits, to defer to its leadership. However, America was never able simply to dictate terms to the world.[4] European influence was important in shaping a framework of economic interdependence and political alliance. U.S. influence over its partners was limited by its strategy: to create a voluntary alliance of self-sustaining, independent, democratic states on the European continent and in Japan. This strategy was brilliantly successful: The trade-off of immediate influence for long-term legitimacy was highly favorable to the United States. As a result of its strategy, however, the United States had, in Geir Lundestad's terms, at best an "empire by invitation"—at least in Europe.[5] In my view, the American "empire" was essentially metaphorical, although American "hegemony"—leadership based on material predominance as well as status—was real.

Third, the decline of American material dominance since 1950 has been significant, but not precipitous. During the 1950s and into the 1960s, the United States controlled a remarkable proportion of the economic resources of the world. U.S. manufacturing production in 1953 was almost double that of the next three leading producers put together (the USSR, Great Britain, and Germany), and its gross national product was more than twice that of Japan and the countries now in the European Community combined.[6] Between 1950 and the end of the 1970s, the U.S. proportion of world product, and of world manufacturing production, fell, but since the mid-to-late 1970s, the American share of world product has been steady at about 23 percent.[7] However, indicators of the U.S. position—high-technology exports—show a deteriorating American position. Taking the early 1950s as a base point, there has indeed been a decline of American power, if we define power not as influence but as "preponderance of material resources."[8] Part of this decline can be interpreted as a reflection of underlying factor endowments, temporarily disrupted outside of North America by World War II and its aftermath. But disturbing trends in productivity and mastery of cutting-edge technologies continue.

Finally, the sources of the challenge to American economic dominance need to be specified carefully. That challenge never came from the Soviet Union, despite what was frequently believed during the height of the Cold War.[9] Since the mid-1970s, the United States has kept pace with Europe but not with Japan in manufacturing production, proportion of world product, and competitiveness in leading high-technology sectors of the economy. The erosion of American material dominance does not result from European, much less Soviet, economic prowess but from a combination of internal political and economic problems, the uniting of Europe, and the remarkable rise of productivity in East Asia.

America's huge public-sector deficits and low private savings rates have combined to make the United States reliant, to an unprecedented degree for a great power, on investment from abroad: Between 1983 and 1990, the United States incurred a cumulative current account deficit of roughly $800 billion. At the same time, a series of well-publicized reports revealed the low academic performance of American secondary school students, which has ominous implications for U.S. competitiveness in future decades. Whether America will retain its ability to compete in sophisticated segments or industries is open to question.[10] For reasons that are hotly debated, Japan and other East Asian countries are the most rapidly growing economies in the world; Japanese firms have, during the past fifteen years, made the most remarkable progress in becoming competitive, or in some cases dominant, in high-technology products.

Thus despite the controversy over the "decline of American hegemony,"[11] the general pattern of power diffusion is clear. U.S. financial strength has been weakened more than its manufacturing productivity or share of world product. Significant relative gains have been made recently only by Japan and East Asian capitalist states, not by Europe (much less by the socialist countries). Europe, however, is a more effective economic actor now than in the 1950s because of the increased size of the European Community and its ability to forge a common economic policy, as indicated by its intransigence on agricultural policy thus far in the Uruguay Round, and by its leadership in policy toward the Soviet Union and Eastern Europe. Thus we can now speak of a tripolar world political economy—with the European Community as the largest entity and East Asia the most rapidly growing one. However, neither Europe nor Japan has the capability to be a political or military leader in the 1990s. A European politician was quoted recently as saying that Europe is "an economic giant, a political dwarf, and a military worm." When one takes into account multiple sources of power, both tangible and intangible, the United States remains the strongest actor in world politics. But the margin of its dominance over Europe and Japan has become slimmer.

IMPLICATIONS FOR POLICY

Charles Krauthammer has recently claimed that the United States is "the only country with the military, diplomatic, political and economic assets to be a decisive player in any conflict in whatever part of the world it chooses to involve itself."[12] The chief error in this assertion is in the word "decisive." The United States has the greatest capacity of any state to intervene on a global basis, although one may doubt that its military power could be effective on the Asian landmass, away from access to its sea power. But its action alone can hardly be decisive, as the war in Vietnam should have taught us. Other states' interests must be engaged along with those of the United States; the United States does not have the ability to create regimes in its image nor, except where it is willing to concentrate a large portion of its resources on a small area, to reshape others' interests through promises of largesse.[13]

John Mearsheimer has argued, quite differently, that hypernationalism in Eastern Europe, the reunification of Germany, and the likely withdrawal of the American "night watchmen" in Europe will lead to intensified political rivalry and perhaps even military conflict among major European powers, essentially as a result of the persistence of anarchy and multipolarity.[14] Mearsheimer places great weight on the fact of anarchy—the absence of centralized enforcement powers on a global basis. In his view, "the distribution and character of military power are the root causes of war and peace" and the collapse of bipolarity in Europe is likely to lead to a more unstable multipolar system. The best remedy, for Mearsheimer, is limited nuclear proliferation: Germany should have a secure nuclear deterrent because "Gemany will feel insecure without nuclear weapons; and Germany's great conventional strength gives it significant capacity to disturb Europe if it feels insecure."[15]

One reason for being skeptical of such realist pessimism is that "anarchy" is a disappointing analytical category because it does not vary. To be analytically meaningful, anarchy must simply mean lack of common government; if anarchy is defined as chaos, it is trivial to show that chaos necessarily accompanies anarchy! Although anarchy in the sense of lack of common government has been a constant throughout the history of the interstate system, cooperation among states has varied substantially. We must therefore look elsewhere to explain variations in the incidence of military conflict.[16] Furthermore, the proliferation of international institutions during the Cold War, and most notably the history of the European Community, show that anarchy does not necessarily prevent cooperation.[17] So Mearsheimer's argument rests on only two props: the alleged effects of multipolarity (resulting both from the end of the Cold War and the decline of American dominance over Europe and Japan) and hypernationalism.

In the absence of stabilizing institutions, multipolarity and hypernationalism are indeed dangerous. States will expect conflict and seek to protect themselves through self-help, as discussed by generations of realist writers. They will seek relative gains; alliances will form in which intra-alliance dynamics may magnify inter-alliance conflict; nationalistic conflicts can set off large-scale war. The scenario is familiar: It is the story of 1914.

In this scenario, expectations play a crucial role. The judgments of leaders depend on their expectations about other states' likely actions. These expectations depend in part on domestic politics and international political structures. Within the realist framework of analysis, expectations are implied to be important because state action is based on rational calculation, which means that leaders seek to maximize subjective expected utility. Rational action in an uncertain world is not fully specified by objective factors; it also depends crucially on expectations.

Focusing on expectations brings us back to institutions. International institutions exist largely because they facilitate self-interested cooperation by reducing uncertainty, thus stabilizing expectations.[18] It follows that the expectations of states will depend in part on the nature and strength of international institutions. Insofar as states regularly follow the rules and standards of international institutions, they signal their willingness to continue patterns of cooperation and therefore reinforce expectations of stability. Doing so does not mean eschewing either one's own interests or the search for influence—indeed, in contemporary Europe, Germany can best acquire both wealth and influence by building European institutions, thus reassuring its partners and preventing the formation of balancing coalitions. Institutions therefore play a crucial role: Insofar as they reassure states about their security, institutions allow governments to emphasize absolute rather than relative gains and therefore maintain the conditions for their own existence. Conversely, when institutions collapse, they are particularly hard to reconstruct because insecure states, seeking relative gains, find it extremely difficult to cooperate sufficiently to build significant international institutions.

So international institutions are key components in a self-reinforcing dynamic of stability—just as their absence or collapse is a key factor in self-reinforcing spirals of hostility and conflict. Notice that this argument assumes that states are self-interested, that they may seek relative as well as absolute gains, and that interdependence can indeed lead to conflict. Even given these classical features of world politics, international institutions help to shape the expectations that shape state behavior. Thus the nature of international institutions in Europe will be crucial to its future peace, and maintaining continuity in institutions is critically important to a peaceful Europe.

From a policy perspective, emphasizing institutions is particularly helpful because they are more responsive to human action than either fundamental political tendencies such as hypernationalism or the international political structures of bipolarity or multipolarity. In my view, avoiding military conflict in Europe after the Cold War depends greatly on whether the next decade is characterized by a continuous pattern of institutionalized cooperation. Will NATO be able to nonantagonistically extend its protection to Eastern Europe, thus inhibiting tendencies toward military buildups in Poland, Czechoslovakia, and Hungary? Will a powerful European Community increasingly attain political as well as economic union and find it possible to at least develop a European foreign policy? Can broader institutions, such as the Conference on Security and Cooperation in Europe (CSCE), be strengthened further in order to give states confidence in others' peaceful intentions toward them? Students of world politics could profit by spending more of their time asking how international institutions should be structured, both within Western and Central Europe and between Europe and other powerful states, in order to prevent the recurrence of a fear-driven slide toward military conflict that would be disastrous for our generation and those to follow.

THE UNITED STATES AND
MULTILATERAL INSTITUTIONS

During the Cold War, the United States exercised leadership and paid the price for it. Indeed, U.S. behavior during the Cold War can be accurately characterized as unconditional leadership. The U.S. leadership not only accepted a world role but also welcomed it, frequently seeking to bolster regimes that would depend on American support rather than offering American support only in reluctant response to requests from foreign governments. Congress and the public occasionally grumbled, but except where the human costs were high, as in Vietnam, they acquiesced.

A continuation of this pattern in the 1990s is unlikely for reasons both of security interests and economic capacity. The collapse of Soviet power in Eastern Europe, and the likely disappearance of the Soviet Union as a superpower seriously threatening American interests, make it hard to argue that American security interests dictate that it continue its role as global policeman. It is the most fundamental principle of foreign policy that a nation's capabilities must be consistent with the interests it seeks to promote and defend. The United States no longer has the economic capabilities to finance such a role itself, especially in view of its internal and external debt burden and political constraints on raising taxation. The habits of hegemony, inculcated in the United States over so many decades, will change. The question is how, and with what effects on world order.

Acting unilaterally, the United States could reduce the scope of its commitments. It could let Europe defend itself against any threats from the Soviet Union—which the Europeans are quite capable, economically and financially, of doing—and let the EC and CSCE, perhaps with modest U.S. backing, cope with strife in Eastern Europe. The United States could adopt a serious domestic energy policy to reduce dependence on the Middle East and withdraw militarily from the Persian Gulf, retaining only a shield of extended deterrence over Israel. It could drastically reduce its military presence in East Asia, leaving its bases in the Philippines without seeking a replacement, and disengaging from its alliances on the Asian mainland. The United States would continue to protect the Japanese archipelago with its nuclear deterrent but would no longer guarantee Japanese access to Persian Gulf oil or to secure supply lines from Europe and the Middle East.

These actions would be consistent with the traditional behavior of great powers defending their own vital interests, but they would be inconsistent with the practices of superpowers, in particular the United States during the past forty years. Some of them, such as the development of an effective domestic energy policy, would be salutary and long overdue. However, restricting the scope of American commitments would also incur serious costs for the United States. As recent events indicate, without extensive U.S. involvement there is a great risk that the determined and aggressive leadership of a well-organized and coherent state, such as Iraq or Iran, could dominate the entire oil-producing area along the Persian Gulf. And without American involvement in Europe, Mearsheimer's gloomy forecast, although by no means inevitable, would become more likely to be realized.

Furthermore, if the United States were to retrench, its influence with its allies or former allies would surely suffer. U.S. economic relations with Europe and Japan would become more difficult to manage; Japan in particular would have less incentive to accommodate American financial markets and the trade demands of the U.S. government. Global issues such as environmental protection would probably be more difficult to cope with in a genuinely multipolar system in which America could not count on deference to its leadership from its allies. Serious domestic adjustments, involving energy conservation and an increase in the domestic savings rate, would almost surely be required; adjustment to more protectionist policies by U.S. trade partners, particularly in Europe, might be necessary. The promised domestic rewards of retrenchment would be unlikely, therefore, to be realized.

In the long run, much could be said for energy conservation and increased savings, but in the short run, forcing painful adjustment onto the American public, via taxes, inflation, or other means of reducing living standards, is costly to politicians. Negative reactions to U.S. policy shifts by its tripolar partners could easily lead to retaliation by the United States and a slide into protectionism, as urged recently, for instance, by the corporate leaders of Chrysler and Ford and by the United Auto Workers.[19] A strategy of retrenchment has risky implications, both at the domestic political level and for long-term national strategy.

A more sensible alternative to the unilateral reduction of American commitments is some form of joint leadership. Under such a system, other states would make much greater contributions to the maintenance of world order, a prosperous international economy, and effective international environmental policies. Not only would

Japan and the European Community make greater contributions; they would have to be willing to take political initiatives—to exercise leadership. For its part, the United States would have to accept that it could not always play the major role in shaping joint policies, nor would its leaders always be at the center of international attention. American willingness to let the European Community take the lead in East European reconstruction is a welcome sign that at least on some issues the Bush administration is beginning to think in terms of joint leadership rather than leader-follower.

Joint leadership requires multilateral institutions. If the United States is to reduce its costly commitments without risking trade wars, it will need to learn how to better use international regimes to further its own policy objectives. Doing so requires building on shared interests where it is feasible for states to gain jointly from cooperation.[20] Where possible, new institutional functions should be assumed by existing organizations because it is usually easier to extend incrementally the activities of an ongoing organization (if it operates relatively well) than to obtain widespread agreement on a new one. Considerable attention needs to be paid to the problem of compliance with rules that can only rarely be obtained through the force of law, although in the European Community law is indeed playing an unexpectedly major role.[21] Effective compliance requires attention to the institutionalization of intergovernmental reciprocity but also, where appropriate, to innovative techniques involving nongovernmental organizations and the use of publicity.[22]

We cannot think clearly about state strategies in contemporary world politics without taking account of the role played by multilateral institutions. As I have argued, European stability is closely linked to institutionalization. And when state strategies change—as those of the United States will have to do during the next decade—multilateral institutions could play a decisive role in cushioning the effects of change and managing the transition to new patterns of leadership to fit changed political and economic structures.

The indispensability of multilateral institutions for joint leadership does not imply that the United States must necessarily rely on the United Nations. International organizations whose members favor antithetical policies can contribute to stalemate rather than to effective action; ineffectiveness can be compounded when the leadership of these organizations is weak and their bureaucracies of low competence. Some elements of the United Nations system have been quite effective, notably the UN Environmental Program, the loosely affiliated World Bank and IMF, and depending on the political conjuncture, the Security Council. Others have had more checkered histories. To recommend that U.S. policy work through multilateral institutions is not to argue that all international organizations are equally worthwhile.[23] It remains to be seen, for example, whether the EC, CSCE, or the UN is the most appropriate institution for coping with the Yugoslav crisis. The EC is the most efficient of these institutions—the most likely to pursue a genuine common policy. Handling the issue in the CSCE would limit the number of participants to states with a direct stake in the issue, and CSCE requires unanimity. Although many of its members do not have a direct stake in the continued existence of Yugoslavia, many of the UN's members do have an indirect stake in the preservation of existing state boundaries. And the UN has an institutional machinery for peacekeeping that CSCE lacks.

Multilateral institutions help governments to deal with fragmented relations of interdependence. But they may also enhance the wisdom of policymaking. Launching interventionist crusades under the United Nations banner would not, in my view, be a great advance. But a great deal could be said for using multilateral institutions to restrain the interventionist impulse in American foreign policy—an impulse all too evident in Lebanon, Nicaragua, and Panama during the past decade. I believe that the United States should retain the unilateral right to use force in the defense of its primary interests—the security of its territory, the autonomy of its governance structures, the livability of its environment, and its capacity to provide a decent standard of living for its citizens. But before it uses force in pursuit of less important interests, it should have to meet a procedural requirement: agreement on action by an appropriate multilateral body that fully represents the governments whose interests were supposedly threatened.

In fall 1990, the United States followed such a procedure for the first time in history: The Bush administration received authorization to use force first from the United Nations Security Council and then from the U.S. Senate. In my view, the process of international debate and discussion was salutary, providing greater legitimacy for American action but also requiring explicit defense of a policy and restraining precipitous action. By including the United Nations Security Council as well as the Senate in the deliberations, the United States institutionalized the principle of intellectual modesty—that no single state, or organization within a state, has a monopoly of foreign policy wisdom. Multilateral institutions should be involved in the foreign policy takeoffs as well as the crash landings. In the 1990s, the United States should be willing to participate in joint leadership with like-minded governments through international institutions. It should also be willing to listen to the views of others.

NOTES

1. Joseph S. Nye, *Bound to Lead: The Changing Nature of American Power* (New York: Basic Books 1990).
2. Barry Buzan, *People, States and Fear,* 2d ed. (Boulder: Lynne Rienner Publishers 1991).
3. For an early, limited discussion of this issue, see Robert O. Keohane, "The Theory of Hegemonic Stability and Changes in International Economic Regimes, 1967–1977," in Ole R. Holsti, Randolph M. Siverson, and Alexander L. George, *Change in the International System* (Boulder: Westview Press 1980), pp. 131–162. The recent debate includes Bruce Russett, "The Mysterious Case of Vanishing Hegemony; or, Is Mark Twain Really Dead?" *International Organization* 39, no. 2 (Spring 1985), pp. 207–232; Robert Gilpin, *The Political Economy of International Relations* (Princeton: Princeton University Press 1987); Paul Kennedy, *The Rise and Fall of the Great Powers* (New York: Random House 1987); and Nye, *Bound to Lead.*
4. Paraphrase, Robert O. Keohane, *After Hegemony: Cooperation and Discord in the World Political Economy* (Princeton: Princeton University Press 1984), p. 177.
5. Geir Lundestad, *The American "Empire"* (Oslo: Norwegian University Press 1990).
6. Bruce Russett, "The Mysterious Case of Vanishing Hegemony," Table 1, p. 212; Keohane, *After Hegemony,* p. 197.
7. Nye, *Bound to Lead,* p. 74.
8. This definition, however crude, is the only one that permits analysts to make nontautological inferences about the effects on patterns of political influence, international cooperation, and changes in patterns of dominance. See Keohane, *After Hegemony,* pp. 32–39.
9. In 1981 Robert Gilpin wrote that "the Soviet Union is, of course, the rising challenger, and it appears to be the one power that in the years to come could supplant the American dominance over the international system" (Robert Gilpin, *War and Change in World Politics* [Cambridge: Cambridge University Press], p. 241).
10. Michael Porter, *The Competitive Advantage of Nations* (New York: Free Press 1990).
11. This debate was started by Paul Kennedy in his seminal work, *The Rise and Fall of the Great Powers: Economic Change and Military Conflict from 1500 to 2000* (New York: Random House 1967). He has been joined, among others, by Davis P. Calleo, *Beyond American Hegemony: The Future of the Western Alliance* (New York: Basic Books 1987), and rebutted by Samuel P. Huntington, "The U.S.—Decline or Renewal," *Foreign Affairs* 67, no. 2 (Winter 1988/89), pp. 76–96; Henry R. Nau, *The Myth of America's Decline: Leading the World Economy into the 1990s* (New York and Oxford: Oxford University Press 1990); and Nye, *Bound to Lead.*

12. Charles Krauthammer, "The Unipolar Moment," *Foreign Affairs* 70, no. 1, "America and the World" 1990/91, p. 24.

13. U.S. policy toward Egypt since the Camp David accords is the most striking counterexample; it is hard to believe that this extremely expensive policy could be duplicated very often, however.

14. John Mearsheimer, "Back to the Future: Instability in Europe after the Cold War," *International Security* 15, no. 2 (Fall 1990), pp. 5–56.

15. Ibid., p. 38. Note the extraordinary personification of Germany in this quotation.

16. Kenneth A. Oye, ed., *Cooperation Under Anarchy* (Princeton: Princeton University Press 1986). For the definition of anarchy, see Robert Axelrod and Robert O. Keohane, "Achieving Cooperation Under Anarchy: Strategies and Institutions," in Kenneth A. Oye, ed., *Cooperation Under Anarchy* (Princeton: Princeton University Press 1986), pp. 226–254.

17. For some pioneering studies of security regimes in Europe, see Volker Rittberger, ed., *International Regimes in East-West Politics* (London: Pinter 1990).

18. Keohane, *After Hegemony,* Chapter 6.

19. *Wall Street Journal,* January 14, 1991, p. B1.

20. Robert O. Keohane and Joseph S. Nye, Jr., "Two Cheers for Multilateralism," *Foreign Policy* 60 (Fall 1985).

21. Federico Mancini, "The Making of a Constitution for Europe," in Robert O. Keohane and Stanley Hoffmann, eds., *The New European Community: Decisionmaking and Institutional Change* (Boulder: Westview Press 1991), Chapter 6.

22. It almost goes without saying that such techniques are more likely to be effective on issues such as the environment, which do not involve immediate security threats and are open to public discussion, than on military security issues. And they are more likely to be efficacious when their targets are democratic rather than authoritarian states. They thus have limited (although not negligible) value.

23. I should note for the sake of clarity that multilateral institutions, in my usage, include informal conventions and formal rules as well as international organizations; institution is therefore a broader category than organization. For a good discussion of changes in international organizations and implications for U.S. policy, see Margaret P. Karns and Karen A. Mingst, eds., *The United States and Multilateral Institutions* (Boston: Unwin Hyman 1990), especially Chapter 11, pp. 289–320.

4

America and Europe in an Era of Revolutionary Change

Stanley Hoffmann

This subject—America and Europe in an era of revolutionary change—is difficult to deal with because these "partners" are undergoing changes that make prediction even more risky than before. Indeed, all the dimensions of the international system are changing at the same time. The Cold War, which was both the relationship of major tension for more than forty years and the framework of a certain kind of order (the rules of the game agreed upon by the superpowers and the hierarchical rules and practices within each camp), is over.

The stage is now dominated not only by economic issues that the writers on the global market and interdependence have been analyzing for some time but also by considerable interstate and above all intrastate turbulence. Issues that promise to be even more unmanageable than the obdurate regional conflicts (in the Middle East, South Africa, and Southwest Asia) that have engendered and been perpetuated by the kinds of arms sales that are currently being denounced, if not yet curtailed, are the reawakening of ethnic issues, the turmoil produced by popular dissatisfaction with tyrannical or corrupt regimes, and the external repercussions of domestic upheavals (such as masses of migrants). It is the combination of economic inequities—in a world where the gap between the rich and the poor countries is growing—and ethnic or religious grievances that is likely to fuel a variety of diffuse conflicts in the years to come.

As I have explained elsewhere,[1] international politics can no longer be analyzed as a "game of states." States remain the key actors of world affairs but are increasingly caught between two other levels: that of the world economy, which has rules, imperatives, and constraints of its own, enforced by a variety of international organizations, and that of the peoples.

The collapse of much of world communism, the need of the former satellites of the Soviet Union in Eastern and Central Europe for outside aid and their desire to be part of the West, and now the desperate plight of the Soviet Union and its republics have reinforced the weight of a global capitalist economy that is made up of millions of decisions and moves by individuals, companies, interest groups, and governments. As for the people, it is impossible to exclude from the study of world affairs their protests against the market's inequities, unpopular or oppressive regimes, and artificial borders that cut across ethnic groups (or force hostile ethnic groups to live together); their frequent capacity to thwart the wills of conquerors; and their ability to disrupt the "game of states" or to impose strategies on the governments of the states. "Structural" theories that look only at the distribution of power among states are bankrupt.

EUROPEAN CONSEQUENCES OF SOVIET TRANSFORMATION

Among the many changes that have revolutionized international relations since 1989, those that have affected two key actors deserve some remarks. The most spectacular change is of course the transformation of the Soviet Union, which is undergoing simultaneously a political revolution, an economic collapse, and the disintegration of first its external and now its internal empires. The combination of creeping bureaucratic and economic paralysis, widespread lack of faith in an ideology whose promises looked more and more remote from drab and corrupt realities, long-repressed but never abolished national and subnational rivalries and hostilities, and Gorbachev's tragic role as a sorcerer's apprentice have resulted in the fall and fragmentation of a superpower that, only a few years ago, many anxious people in the West saw as ten feet tall and as a potential military master of the world. We have been rudely reminded of the fact that military might without a sound economic base and without adequate popular will and morale is nothing but a facade.

As a result, what Western statesmen had gotten used to considering as a weakened and increasingly cooperative major actor has become a subject of uncertainty and anxiety because its very future as an actor is in doubt and because all the alternatives to a revamped union—whether it be a weak confederation or a set of would-be sovereign nations—seem dangerous and unmanageable.

This has been the situation especially since the failed coup of August 19–21, 1991, which further accelerated the speed of events that was already too fast for commentators and statesmen alike. The Gorbachev years, 1985–1991, may well appear in history books as a brief, happy transition between two opposite "Soviet dangers"—the superpower threat of the Cold War years and the disintegrating, unstable, and unpredictable threat of imperial, political, and economic unraveling. The ability of any international system to cope with revolution in one of the major actors has never been edifying, and the scope—geographic and functional—of the Soviet revolution exceeds that of previous examples in history.

As a result of these cataclysmic events, Germany has suddenly been transformed from a middle power contained in a variety of constraining structures and institutions—such as the Cold War, NATO, and the EC—into a major actor, thanks to its unification, its economic potential (once the absorption of the former GDR into the Federal Republic has been completed), and its geographic position. Within the EC, the relative equilibrium among the "big three"— France, the Federal Republic, and Britain—has been broken in Germany's favor. Hence there are two convergent if contradictory fears that the new Germany might dominate the EC (compare the power of the Bundesbank to shape the economic policies and employment situations of Germany's partners in the EMS [European Monetary System]) or that Germany might emancipate itself from the constraints of the Community. NATO is still there but has lost its enemy, and within it, Germany might soon be the most important military factor on the continent, given the likely removal of American forces and the unilateral destruction of NATO's tactical nuclear arsenal. Above all, between Germany and Japan (the old allies of the Axis) there is now no single great power. This might change if, by miracle, a new post–Soviet Union emerges or if an independent Russia consolidates its own political, economic, and military resources, but such a prospect is *Zukunftsmusik* (a castle in the air).

Here again are dual fears: that Germany might be tempted to play a major diplomatic and economic role in the affairs of the countries to its east, as a newly self-confident national state with an external policy and ambitions of its own, and that Germany, inhibited by its recent reticent past, will fail to play a role in world affairs commensurate with its power and thus prevent the emergence of Europe as a key actor in a world that needs steering, especially now that the USSR is a stake rather than a great power, that Japan continues to often hide behind the United States in the world's noneconomic affairs, and that the capacity of the United States to shape the international system declines. Those who fear German "renationalization" point to Bonn's policy in the Yugoslav drama; those who fear German passivity evoke the Gulf War.

AMERICAN DISORIENTATION

Neither the United States nor Europe is well prepared for the world that is appearing now. The United States sees itself (I am referring here to the general public as well as to the elites) as the only superpower. Before August 1991 the spectacular difficulties of the USSR, the extraordinary changes in its foreign and defense policies and structures, its need for external assistance, the improbability of any Soviet resort to force outside the borders of the USSR—and therefore the neutralization of its one remaining "card" as a major power—had been noted with satisfaction (and remarkably little *Schadenfreude* [malicious glee]) in the United States. So has the unwillingness of the two biggest economic competitors of Washington, Germany and Japan, to develop an active noneconomic *Weltpolitik* (international strategy).

However, despite these facts, despite the military triumph of the United States in the Gulf War, and however much members of the American establishment endorse and reassure themselves with my friend Joseph Nye's arguments in his thoughtful book *Bound to Lead*,[2] there is a strong undercurrent of disorientation.

On the one hand, even in the Middle East the difficulty of translating military might into political success remains formidable—if by political success one means more than procedural gains. Saddam Hussein is still around and the Palestinian question is still unresolved. On the other hand, the domestic problems of the United States have continued to mount, the trade and budget deficits are still there, and there are many different voices arguing, both from the democratic Left and from the conservative Right, for a shift in priorities.

Now that the United States is no longer challenged in its physical security by any other power, why should Washington continue to carry the burdens of world leadership? Why not let its economic competitors face the choice between carrying them now and chaos? Why not finally deal with issues—such as education, race, drugs, cities, the rate of savings, and the troubles of the banking system—which, left unattended, will erode American power abroad, just as the inefficiency of the Soviet economy had undermined Soviet power?

Already the reluctance of the U.S. government to play a major role in the rehabilitation of Eastern and Central Europe, to contribute more than technical assistance and a few minor measures of help to Moscow, and the way in which the Bush administration demanded that its allies cover the bulk of the costs of the Gulf War show that the new era of "unipolarity" is highly paradoxical. The single superpower has clay feet and a flat purse.

The diplomatic activism displayed by the administration in 1991 was partly a shrewd attempt at exploiting the image of a victorious great power while this image had a shadow, partly an effort at compensating for the decline of one of the two great instruments of American power—economic assistance—and for the dilemmas entailed by the use of the other great instrument—arms sales—at a time when the Cold War is no more and when such sales risk fueling disastrous regional conflicts. Diplomatic activism simply reflected in part the reluctance of George Bush and his team to address domestic issues. People suspicious, now and forever, of American imperialism are likely to see in this agitation new evidence of America's will to shape the world. But others may see it more as a *combat d'arrière-garde,* a way of covering a retreat, or of minimizing its costs.

EUROPEAN UNCERTAINTY

The European uncertainty is of a different order. On the one hand, the European Community faces more seriously than ever before the problem of becoming not merely a wealthy integrated market and thus a single actor in the world economy but a political entity in the two essential dimensions of politics: internally, by developing more federal-like institutions and a genuinely "European" electorate, and externally, by producing a common diplomacy and security policy.

On the other hand, the new Europe without its iron curtain and Berlin Wall remains a divided continent—the new division being between its richer and democratic Western half and an Eastern half that is still groping toward capitalism and democracy. The two issues are not separable: many in the Community, who want it to become a kind of "United States of Europe," believe that such "deepening" must be given priority over any large-scale enlargement of the EC, and many of those who still prefer a "Europe of states" argue that an enlargement is the only way of not frustrating the hopes and expectations of the ex-Communist countries—and of not having to face the prospects of an "invasion" by the dispossessed coming from the East.

The trouble is, indeed, that on every topic there are deep divisions among the members of the EC. America's European allies are still far from constituting a "second pillar" and from speaking with a single voice, as is shown in the fiasco of the attempt at a common stand in the Gulf War; the difficulties encountered by the Twelve when they tried to deal with the Yugoslav drama; the multiple viewpoints on institutional reform; the failure of François Mitterrand's attempt to find a halfway house, called confederation, between "deepening" and "enlargement" (because the Czechs, Poles, and Hungarians reject any halfway house that might become a permanent one); the reluctance of both Britain (overtly) and Germany (more subtly) to endorse the French call for a common security policy that would, in effect, put the West European Union (WEU) ahead of NATO (and, it must be added, the absence of any indication that France itself would abandon its stance of military autonomy); and even the uncertainty about the timing and modalities of monetary union.

In this period of transition (but toward what?), two things are striking when one looks at U.S.-European relations. One is what might be called a certain "normalization" of these relations, as seen from Western Europe. For the members of the Community—except perhaps Britain—the United States is certainly a major partner (and competitor) but no longer the dominant power that it was in the days of the Cold War and before the European *relance* of the late 1980s.

This explains why American pressures (for instance against the Common Agricultural Policy or the Airbus) and injunctions (against any moves in the realm of defense that could detract from NATO) are greeted now with greater indifference, or even determination to resist, than in earlier periods. The unification of Germany, its economic dynamism (which the economic difficulties of integrating the former GDR into the Federal Republic are not likely to impair for long), and its own rapprochement with Moscow have reduced the leverage Washington had for so long over Bonn. Franco-American relations, despite French participation in the Gulf War, remain as ticklish as ever. Only the British government remains unwilling to compromise the "special relations" it believes exist with the United States, and even it is torn between the American bond and the desire to take part, however tepidly, in the development of the EC. For the Community, America has become an "ordinary power";[3] the exception to this normalization was the Gulf War, but few people expect similar displays of American military uniqueness in other parts of the globe in coming years.

The second striking feature is far less original. It is a trait that has characterized U.S. policy for a long time indeed: ambivalence toward European unification. American officials, at times, talk as if the new entity that is emerging on the other side of the Atlantic was likely to become a dangerous rival, especially in the economic realm (hence all the handwringing and anxieties about "fortress Europe") but also insofar as a revived WEU could challenge NATO's supremacy (hence the speed with which the American administration, with British help, obtained a reorganization of NATO's force structure and a proclamation of NATO's eminence).

At other moments, it is not West European unity but West European inability to unite and to speak with a single voice that seems to annoy and to worry Americans. Those, like John Mearsheimer,[4] who predict that a post–Cold War Europe will revert to the interstate and intrastate conflicts of pre-1914 Europe, that Germany will again either feel insecure or make its neighbors feel insecure, and that as the result of European follies the United States might once more have to send its boys to rescue the old continent from itself are afraid not of a change toward unity but of a return to the past. This fear, of course, converges with its opposite in one respect: It too can be used to justify the perpetuation of a NATO dominated by the United States.

There is something artificial on both sides of the Atlantic about the debate on security. West Europeans are far from being able to challenge NATO's supremacy, not only because they do not agree on a European security or defense policy (especially not insofar as operations outside of Western Europe are concerned) but also because their own priorities, at present, are anything but military—which explains why, in effect, the military status quo is perfectly acceptable to France as well as to Britain and Germany.

As for Americans, the "victories" obtained in 1991 with respect to NATO may turn out to be Pyrrhic, for it is difficult to see where the new multinational forces and the Rapid Reaction Force to be established are likely to be used, given the disappearance of a Soviet threat (even against Eastern Europe) and the continuing reluctance of several European members of NATO to fight "out of area" (or in Eastern Europe). Moreover, the reduction of American troops and armaments in Europe cannot but, in the long run, affect America's domination of the military alliance.

PROSPECTS FOR EUROPE

The years to come are likely to see increasing West European economic and diplomatic involvement in Eastern Europe—an area almost abandoned to the EC by Washington—and in the former Soviet Union, to which the Community is likely to become a partner at least as important as the United States, which is economically more reticent. We are also likely to see many fights, warning shots, deterrent postures, charges and countercharges, and, finally, compromises between the EC and the United States in economic matters. But the military security issue is more likely to remain dormant until all the uncertainties mentioned here have begun to dissipate.

This does not mean that the upheavals that might accompany the disintegration of the Soviet Union and particularly the claims and counterclaims of nationalities seeking independence and attracted by all the trappings of sovereignty could not create threats for the East European neighbors of Russia, Belorussia, Ukraine, Moldavia, and others. What if a free Ukraine claims parts of Slovakia, for instance? But it is difficult to imagine a large-scale military involvement of the West Europeans (or the Americans) even more than in the case of Yugoslavia. It is likely that the efforts of the EC countries and of the CSCE will aim more at providing procedures of conciliation and good offices and at using whatever economic aid will be made available as an instrument of peace.

The insecurities of Europe will result more from the problem of refugees seeking asylum or immigrants fleeing economic collapse; from the economic plight and political difficulties of the new would-be capitalist democracies in Eastern and Central Europe; from the temptation some of the West European actors might have to bestow diplomatic favors on different ex-Soviet republics; and from the gap between the well-institutionalized Western half and the far more chaotic Eastern and ex-Soviet parts of Europe. These are issues that will be very difficult for the Europeans to handle well and for the solution of which the United States appears singularly unprepared and uninvolved.

NOTES

1. See Stanley Hoffmann, "A New World and Its Troubles," in Nicholas X. Rizopoulos, ed., *Sea-Changes* (New York: Council on Foreign Relations 1990), pp. 274–292.

2. Joseph S. Nye, *Bound to Lead: The Changing Nature of American Power* (New York: Basic Books 1990).

3. See Richard Rosecrance's definition in his *America as an Ordinary Country* (Ithaca: Cornell University Press 1976).

4. See John Mearsheimer's "Back to the Future: Instability in Europe After the Cold War," *International Security* 15, no. 1 (Summer 1990), pp. 5–56.

5

Two-Level Games:
The Impact of Domestic Politics
on Transatlantic Bargaining

Robert D. Putnam

We peer into the future as we celebrate the end of the Cold War. How will the dramatic changes in East-West relations, symbolized by the collapse of the Berlin Wall and formalized in the Paris summit of November 1990, affect the relationship between Europe and the United States? Predictions of the future are notoriously difficult; it is best to begin with a glance at the past.

The pace of history in 1989 and 1990 was extraordinary. On November 28, 1989, Chancellor Helmut Kohl made his first public proposal for German unification. "How a reunited Germany would ultimately look," he said rather tentatively, "no one knows today."[1] In less than a year, we knew. On that same day in November 1989, the Communist party in Czechoslovakia surrendered its powers to a two-week-old opposition party headed by an unsung playwright. The triumphant liberation of Eastern Europe evoked the stirring "Prisoners' Chorus" at the end of the first act of Beethoven's *Fidelio*, but that was, after all, only the first act. The transformations of 1989 and 1990 did not herald the arrival of a tranquil new millennium or the end of history. Each day's headlines from the East over the ensuing months reminded us of the dangers ahead. Nevertheless, the revolutions of 1989 and 1990 represented an extraordinary success for postwar Western foreign policy.

Four decades earlier, twelve war-weary nations had signed the North Atlantic Treaty, creating an alliance that has already kept the peace in Europe far longer than the structures created by Metternich or Bismarck. Despite the ups and downs of the economic cycle, these four decades of Atlantic partnership also witnessed the most rapid and sustained period of economic growth in Europe's history. If peace and prosperity are the two highest objectives of any statesman, the founders of the alliance on both sides of the Atlantic succeeded beyond their wildest hopes. And yet John F. Kennedy warned at Paulskirche in Frankfurt in 1963 that "our liberty is endangered if we rest on our achievements. For time and the world do not stand still. Change is the law of life. And those who look only to the past are certain to miss the future."[2]

FOREIGN AFFAIRS AND DOMESTIC POLITICS

Facing a voyage on uncharted seas, the wise seaman uses several different methods of navigation, both familiar tools tested by time and innovative techniques promising new insights. Similarly, for a comprehensive assessment of the future of U.S.-Europe relations in a post–Cold War world we should seek a blend of older and newer conceptual approaches. Following the precepts of realist theories of international relations, for example, it would be useful to reexamine the basic geopolitical interests of the major nations. Or, to take another illustration, it would be instructive to consider historical patterns of alignment and realignment in the aftermath of analogous epochs of imperial decline and revolutionary change.

In evaluating and forecasting relations among modern democracies, however, it is also important to pay special attention to the interconnections between foreign affairs and domestic politics. That is the subject of this chapter. Traditionally, we have thought of international diplomacy as a kind of chess game, but in an increasingly interdependent world, particularly among democratic states, we need to think of each national leader as playing a kind of "two-level game."

Across the international table from each leader sit foreign counterparts, and around a second table behind this leader sit spokespersons for key domestic interests—business, labor, legislators, coalition partners, "public opinion," and so on. What makes this two-level game so complex is that each leader must try to find a successful and consistent strategy at both tables simultaneously. Actions that are rational at one table (such as deploying new weapons or subsidizing weak industries) may be impolitic for that same player at the other table. Nevertheless, there are powerful incentives for consistency between the two games. Neither of the two games can be ignored by central decisionmakers as long as their countries remain interdependent yet sovereign democracies.

In particular, this theory suggests that all major actions by each leader at the international table, both threats and promises, must be "ratified" by that leader's key domestic constituencies. (In an earlier version of this theory that concentrated on international cooperation,[3] I emphasized the need to ratify international agreements, but in my later work[4] this notion of "ratification" was extended to suggest that credible international threats must also win domestic approval. To take a simple example, for some years after the Vietnam debacle, America's public would not support hostile action. Saddam Hussein's refusal to withdraw from Kuwait was predicated in part on the belief that the U.S. threat of war would not be "ratified" by the American public.) In some cases, particularly involving formal international agreements, ratification may be constitutionally required, most commonly by the national legislature. However, I am here using the term "ratification" in a much broader sense to refer to the need to win domestic support, formal or informal, tacit or explicit, for international initiatives. This need for domestic ratification is the crucial link between the two games.

The stringency of this requirement varies, of course, from domain to domain, from time to time, and from country to country, depending on the institutional and social structure and political culture. Presidents of the V. Republic of France, for example, are granted considerable leeway in security policy, and the degree of congressional consent required for military moves by the U.S. administration under the War Powers Act has been a matter of some controversy in recent years. Nevertheless, the foreign policy autonomy of the heads of government in the Atlantic democracies is generally circumscribed in ways that make this "two-level game" metaphor a useful analytic lens for understanding their behavior.

Often the stakes in the domestic game are more important to the national leader than the international stakes, and often the stakes at the two tables are linked, so a victory at one table may produce gains at the other table and vice versa. Thus, any prudent foreign policy maker must be Janus-faced. Yet the leader is not a passive cipher, merely registering the parallelogram of forces in the two arenas. Rather, the leader typically acts strategically, seeking opportunities for synergistic gains at both tables simultaneously. In this sense, the two-level game approach is not a purely "bottom-up" theory of the domestic roots of foreign policy, for the leader acts with some degree of autonomy. Foreign policy in this view is not constituency driven, but it is constituency constrained.

Using this two-level game image of international affairs, in this essay I explore the domestic dimensions of American foreign policy, writing primarily as an American about America, although I also hazard some judgments about European trends in the wake of the Cold War. I shall turn later to U.S.-European economic issues, which I believe to be more problematical than security issues, but I want to begin with U.S. security relations, where domestic politics is no less relevant. After all, the Versailles Treaty failed because the U.S. president acted out of step with opinion back home, a classic example of failed domestic ratification of a major international development. Domestic politics on both sides of the Atlantic also paved the way for the tragedies of 1933–1945, and among those Europeans and Americans who together created the remarkable postwar Western institutional arrangements, fear of resurgent American isolation was a central motivation.

The Atlantic partnership was triggered by the palpable threat to the common security of America and Western Europe posed by the military power of the Soviet Union. Shared democratic ideals were also important to the alliance (I do not endorse the *Realpolitik* view that values are irrelevant in international affairs), but in 1947 and 1948 one did not need to be an idealistic internationalist nor a fervent anti-Communist to see that the countries that signed the North Atlantic Treaty shared a common interest in deterring further Soviet expansion. The clarity of this shared interest convinced even American isolationists like Sen. Arthur H. Vandenberg to reverse a centuries-old American fear of foreign entanglements.

That common threat is now gone, probably not to recur in my lifetime. Opinions differ about the future of the Soviet Union. Some believe that it has no future at all, at least in the sense of a unified state—that the collapse of the Soviet empire that began in Berlin will ultimately lead to disintegration of the Soviet Union itself or at least its descent into chronic civil war. Others believe that hard-liners in the KGB and the Red Army may reassert authoritarian rule and impose a sullen order on the rebellious republics. But whatever the future holds for Mikhail Gorbachev and his successors, it seems highly unlikely that within the foreseeable future they will be able to pose a threat to the security of Western Europe comparable to that which gave rise to the Atlantic Alliance.

DOMESTIC POLITICS
IN THE UNITED STATES

Against this historical background, what are the views of the domestic U.S. audiences that are relevant to our security arrangements with Europe? Here we should look not for specific guidance on detailed questions of military strategy and diplomacy, such as the definition of "the NATO area" or the role of the Conference on Security and Cooperation in Europe (CSCE), but rather for broad attitudes toward American engagement in European security that will constrain American decisionmakers as they seek domestic ratification for their moves at the international chessboard.

What was the U.S. public mood as the Cold War ended? In 1990 most Americans saw our country slipping in comparison to our allies, but even before the victories of the Persian Gulf in 1991 Americans did not betray a feeling of collapse, either of power or of will. A survey in spring 1990 showed that by a 75:22 percent margin Americans believed the United States to be in decline economically as compared with Europe and Asia. But Americans blamed ourselves for this decline—33 percent blamed U.S. business, 28 percent blamed the U.S. government, and 19 percent blamed U.S. workers, whereas only 14 percent blamed Japan and 3 percent blamed Europe.[5] Polls revealed a strong desire for the so-called peace dividend and anxiety about the sluggish responsiveness of domestic institutions. The American public agreed with most foreign commentators that the U.S. slippage was caused by domestic failings and must be corrected by domestic policy changes. And the decline was not to be exaggerated, for the scale of the U.S. economy remains enormous: Roughly every twenty-eight months growth in the United States adds the equivalent of another Spain to the size of our economy.[6]

To be sure, in the 1990s growing numbers of Americans would like to invest more of their energies at home, addressing long-deferred and costly domestic problems such as education, health care, poverty, and physical infrastructure. The rising budget deficit and a long-standing desire for alliance burden sharing both reflected and encouraged this mood. The modest U.S. contribution to East European recovery—more symbolic than substantial—seemed constrained by domestic economic limits. When President Bush visited Czechoslovakia in October 1990, the only thing he donated was a replica of the American Liberty Bell, and at the London G-7 summit of 1991 he was visibly more reluctant than his European interlocutors were to offer tangible economic aid to the Soviet Union. This failure to invest in the consolidation of the victory of the West's postwar strategy strikes many Americans (including me) as a short-sighted failure of leadership on the part of the administration. At the same time, the administration's reluctance authentically represented a national feeling that following the end of the Cold War the realities of American foreign policy would rest on (as President Bush said in another context) "more will than wallet."[7]

Nevertheless, a surprising air of liberal internationalism persists in America today, along with a continuing aspiration to play a leading role in world affairs. By 1990 (even before the Gulf War), two-thirds of all Americans said that America should play a more active role in the world, a proportion that has actually risen in recent years.[8] The widespread desire to address domestic concerns was not a kind of neoisolationism. Against this backdrop, the readiness of Congress and the public to support the administration's firm resistance to Saddam Hussein was not surprising. In short, Americans believe that they have been falling behind and that they need to get their own house in order, but surprisingly few want to abdicate the role of world leadership that the United States has played for as long as most of us can remember.

U.S. FOREIGN POLICY TOWARD EUROPE

What does this pattern of attitudes mean for American public support for the partnership with Europe? The long decades of Atlantic partnership have left a strong sense among Americans that, as Catherine Kelleher has put it,[9] Europeans are part of "us" (Americans), that is, part of a broader Western community. These years have wrought a powerful transformation of American attitudes to foreign policy. In particular, American confidence in a stronger, unified Germany is high. Only one in every ten Americans opposed German unification, and only two in ten consider reunified Germany a threat to world peace[10]—much smaller minorities of skeptics than in most of Germany's European neighbors. Furthermore, Americans are not eager to pull out of their NATO partnership; three-quarters of American voters say that the United States should keep some troops in Europe indefinitely, whereas only 18 percent would prefer to withdraw entirely.

Our troop strength will decline, and appropriately so—probably even below the force levels agreed in Paris in November 1990. As the threat from the East diminishes, the need for the U.S. counterbalance will also decline, and Americans have no desire to be seen as an "occupying power" in Germany. American domestic economic problems will also make cost-saving troop reductions attractive. The only development I can foresee that might lead to a rupture of the transatlantic security relationship comes not from American neoisolationism but from changes in European attitudes, for European statesmen, too, need continuing domestic ratification (if only tacit) for the Atlantic Alliance.

COMPATIBILITY OF DOMESTIC POLITICS IN EUROPE AND THE UNITED STATES?

European trends are harder for me to assess, but my sense is that Germany will have larger ambitions, more confidence, and probably a more assertive, critical attitude toward the United States and a more attentive interest in Europe's Eastern neighbors. Seen from America, Europe itself seems more self-reliant and self-confident than at any time since World War II because of the optimism of Europe 1992, brighter prospects for competing with the United States, a nearly vanished threat from the East, and, with new leadership in Britain, the prospect of smoother progress toward European unity. Even if this mood should darken somewhat in the years ahead, American peculiarities and insensitivities may well seem less tolerable to a more self-reliant Europe. Conversely, Americans' readiness to remain in Europe would change overnight if a German government were to suggest that the United States had overstayed its welcome.

Nevertheless, my best guess is that the United States will continue to be seen as a useful balance wheel by most Europeans, including most Germans. The most likely changes in the European security situation, such as worsening ethnic conflict or authoritarian reaction in Eastern Europe or the USSR, would probably reinvigorate Atlantic unity and the sense of stability that it has provided. Viewed strictly within Europe, American and European security interests are actually less divergent today than during the four decades of extended nuclear deterrence that gave rise to recurrent crises from flexible response to Euromissiles. No longer do Atlantic leaders need to worry about weighing the security of Hamburg against that of Chicago. As the Gulf crisis reminds us, transatlantic conflict is more likely to arise over what we used to call "out-of-area" threats—that is, crises in the Third World, particularly if the Israeli-Palestinian problem becomes more heated. Yet within America public opinion is far from united on these Third World issues, and the same is probably true for Europe. Political differences are more likely to cut across the Atlantic divide than to reinforce that divide. Regarding balance, I do not expect that Third World issues, taken alone, would cause the breakup of the alliance.

The United States must continue to underwrite European stability, both as an ultimate counterweight to Soviet power and as a reassuring presence. America might be looked upon as an interested party with a relatively detached perspective, more comfortable with a stronger Germany than are Germany's nearer neighbors and a credible stabilizer in Soviet eyes. America's most significant challenge is to forgo command-style leadership for a more subtle role. The United States will need to accept a new, more complex role in Europe: not as uncle, but as brother or perhaps cousin. Nevertheless, unless there is more assertive truculence on the European side than I can now foresee, the American public will probably accept the new family arrangement, perhaps even more readily than will the American establishment. In short, the risks of ingrown isolationism are to my mind less on the American side than on the European side.

All in all, on political-military issues, I see no serious domestic threats to continuing Atlantic partnership. However, the Soviet threat will not provide such a powerful glue for the Atlantic partnership in the future as it has in the past. Economic frictions may thus become more damaging than in the past, so let me turn now to the underlying structure of the political economy of European-American relations.

DIVERGING TRENDS: ECONOMIC INTEGRATION AND POLITICAL FRAGMENTATION

The future of the world political economy will be determined by the tension between two fundamental imperatives: the powerful steady trend toward global economic integration and the equally powerful persistence of political fragmentation.

On any political map of the world, virtually all the borders are as clear today as ever. To be sure, inside Western Europe the boundaries may perhaps become slightly fainter in the years ahead, but elsewhere in the world—above all, within Eastern Europe and the Soviet Union—political boundaries are actually becoming more distinct.

By sharp contrast, on an economic map of the world showing the real flows of financial and commercial activity, national boundaries are disappearing. Companies at the frontier of economic development, such as Daimler-Benz, Mitsubishi, IBM, and many other firms in the "trilateral world" of Europe, America, and East Asia, buy and sell, develop, produce, and market their goods and services, raise and invest their capital, and plan their strategies virtually without regard to national boundaries. Is

Ford really an American company, Honda a Japanese company, Adidas a German company? Sped by the microelectronic and telecommunications revolutions, information and capital flow instantaneously around the world in an ever denser web of interdependence.

Global market integration has created unprecedented prosperity. Economies that are fully enmeshed in it have grown rapidly, however poor their stock of natural resources and however large or small their domestic market. Look at Singapore or Taiwan, for example. In contrast, economies that have remained autarkic, such as the Soviet Union, have fallen further and further behind, however great their natural advantages. Those who exclude themselves from this global web of interdependence pay a very heavy price.

However, interdependence has also created a dilemma for governments. The openness of economies means that the policy levers available to public officials don't work as effectively as they used to: When a government steps on the fiscal or monetary accelerator, it is the automobile in the next lane that speeds up. Conversely, more of what happens within each economy is determined, perhaps inadvertently, by decisions taken in other nations. Now more than ever, the electoral fate of a member of Congress in Ohio depends on decisions taken in Yokohama or Stuttgart, and the fate of a European government's economic policy depends in part on decisions taken (or not taken) by the U.S. Congress or the Federal Reserve. In short, politics in different countries are becoming more and more entangled across political boundaries.

These twin facts—that our markets have become increasingly global while our politics remain parochial—have powerful consequences for international affairs. Here the two-level game metaphor is even more apt and the entanglements between the two levels even more intimate and constant. Neither George Bush nor Helmut Kohl can pledge free trade to his international colleagues while pledging protectionism at home—or at least he cannot keep both pledges. Often countries would be better off if they could make deals internationally, but striking an international deal without upsetting some of the domestic games in the process is not easy.

PLAYING TWO-LEVEL GAMES
MORE EFFECTIVELY: THE SIGNIFICANCE
OF PERSONAL LEADERSHIP

Two-level games are particularly difficult to play successfully when, as is often the case, the gains from international cooperation are widespread but diffuse (like lower prices to consumers) and the costs are concentrated on a particular social sector (such as the producers in an inefficient firm). In this case, veto groups may be able to block even an agreement that would serve the interests of most people in every country. Issues of this sort may become ever more common as interdependence proceeds. A prominent contemporary example is the GATT Uruguay Round, the denouement of which was postponed in disarray in December 1990.

These trade talks are an important test of how effectively Europe and the United States can play two-level games in a post–Cold War world. At the international table, the future of the global economy into the twenty-first century is at stake: $100 billion a year in world trade or, conversely, the potential for a wave of worldwide protectionism and a retreat into regional trading blocs in Europe, East Asia, and the Americas. Already we can see in the North American Free Trade Area negotiations between Canada, Mexico, and the United States, the implementation of the Europe 1992 initiatives, and discussions among the major Pacific powers the kernels of an alternative, less multilateral, and perhaps less stable global trading system. In this alternative future, the cooperative "trilateral world" that has been managed reasonably smoothly (for example, through the G-7 summits) over the past several decades would be replaced by a new, more antagonistic "tripolar world," in which Europe (led by Germany), East Asia (led by Japan), and the Americas (led by the United States) jostle each other uneasily for predomination.

The Uruguay Round talks have taken place among the 107 nations since 1986, but their fate comes down to what happens with Europe's farm protectionism in Brussels. If the EC were unable to offer an acceptable proposal to reduce its $125-billion-a-year agricultural subsidy programs, the agreements that have been reached during the GATT talks—in tariff reduction, services, intellectual property, foreign investment, and other currently protected areas— would be in jeopardy. A secondary complication has arisen at the American domestic table, where certain firms have blocked progress on liberalizing the service sector. However, even most European commentators believe that this issue is much less crucial to success than the agricultural question.

The European domestic tables do not bode well for agreement because of the domestic political interests of Chancellor Kohl and President Mitterrand. Farmers wield far more political muscle in Germany and France than they do in America. The European Community's Common Agricultural Policy costs European taxpayers $100 billion annually ($1,400 for a family of four) and costs all other industrial nations $250 billion a year.[11] Yet most of those people around the world whose economic future depends on the outcome are unable to vote in the crucial European elections. Of course, this sense of disenfranchisement simply mirrors that felt by Europeans when they have to endure a macroeconomic policy that is "made in America." Moreover, just as many Americans have sympathized with European criticisms of administration policy, so also many Europeans sympathize with foreign criticisms of the Common Agricultural Policy. These crosscutting patterns of alignment and misalignment are the inevitable consequence of the mismatch between global economics and parochial politics.

The two-level game metaphor calls special attention to the role of the chief executive, forced to balance and integrate domestic and international concerns. This metaphor contrasts with two traditional logics of international affairs. In the logic of realism, the international table is dominant, and the chief executive is merely an automaton, responding to the dictates of the international system. In the second logic of what one American theorist calls "domesticism," domestic politics have primacy, and the chief executive is simply a passive agent, registering the net vector of domestic forces and moving in the indicated direction.

However, if the two logics do not correspond—and in the new world of global interdependence, they will increasingly fail to correspond—then the chief executive must choose how to meld them. The fundamental question of market integration versus political disintegration will be resolved largely by the skill and strength of our political leaders. Playing two-level games requires strong leaders: someone to resolve domestic conflicts, to seek trade-offs among competing domestic interests and make decisions stick. Conversely, the greater the power of minority interests (or veto groups) in the ratification process, the greater the likelihood of international conflict.

Concerning the Atlantic political economy of the 1990s, the most serious risk that I see for the future is the possibility of deadlock at the domestic table with a weak executive who simply externalizes that deadlock. Familiarity with international issues and a fine-tuned sensitivity to the interweaving of domestic and foreign politics will be increasingly important. Even less important than the leader's personal characteristics and professional qualifications are the institutional factors that enable that leader to overcome narrower pressures in favor of broader constituencies.

On the American side, the constitutional separation of powers between Congress and the president, the weakness of the political parties, and the increasing power of narrow interests can cause gridlock. There is a gathering debate in the United States today about the performance of its government, a growing sense that American democratic institutions are faltering just at the moment of greatest international triumph for its democratic ideals. The potential for irresponsible action and inaction by political leaders is troubling. It may well cause growing difficulties in transatlantic relations, as it already has in the case of the U.S. budget deficit.

In recent decades, partisan division has been superimposed onto the constitutional separation of powers. Between 1900 and 1952 there were only eight years in which Congress and the presidency were controlled by different parties, whereas since 1952 the United States has seen divided government more than two-thirds of the time. Moreover, changes in congressional procedures and in election campaigning have weakened the capacity of leaders to aggregate interests and overcome partisan gridlock. A new generation of individually entrepreneurial politicians has emerged, and the number of organized interest groups has burgeoned. The new system does provide a kind of microresponsiveness, but the new leaders and groups represent narrower selves, and they escape accountability for the overall pattern of public policy. In short, this system shortchanges broader interests at the expense of narrower ones, and stalemate becomes more common. These trends help explain the growing discontent of Americans with their political system, and they will also complicate the task of solving transatlantic two-level games.

On the European side, we must recognize, first of all, that the game has not just two levels but three. At the first, the global level (illustrated by the GATT negotiations in Geneva, for example), the European Community negotiates with other states, including the United States. At the second, the Community level (symbolized by the Brussels Article 133 committee, for example), representatives of the member states negotiate with one another to determine the Community's stance in the global negotiations. At the third, the national level (exemplified by a cabinet meeting on Downing Street or the *Bundeskanzleramt*), national leaders negotiate to determine their position in the Community-level negotiations, with agricultural ministers or the FDP (Free Democratic Party) pitted against the CDU (Christian Democratic Union). And as if these complications were not enough, there can be yet further negotiations nested inside these three, as illustrated by John Major's domestic difficulties with Margaret Thatcher during the run-up to Maastricht. At each stage, the risks posed by veto groups or weak leadership rise exponentially.

As the Community becomes more integrated, Europeans seem ever more reluctant to risk their hard-won internal agreements in the give-and-take of Atlantic negotiation. If European unity means that Europeans more and more present "take-it-or-leave-it" positions based on domestic veto-group politics, as happened in the GATT negotiations, then Atlantic conflicts are sure to increase. I am more fearful of a partially integrated, weakly led Europe than I am of a strong Europe that can rise above parochial domestic interests. The unification of Germany might seem to suggest that the *Bundeskanzler* should become de facto the principal spokesperson for Europe, but history makes that unlikely to be acceptable to other Europeans. The unelected European Commission lacks the necessary democratic legitimacy. Many Americans sympathize with European critics of the "democracy deficit" in the European institutions, but if the European Parliament were to gain increased powers of blockage without at the same time acquiring more coherent leadership, transatlantic tensions might well be exacerbated. Transatlantic cooperation in the years ahead is at serious risk unless Europe moves more quickly toward a genuine federal system with a chief executive who can resolve the conflicts among the three tables.

The issue here is not simply a trade-off between political participation and political leadership, between democratic legitimacy and decision-making authority. Rather it is between microresponsiveness on the one hand and accountability to more inclusive constituencies on the other. In that sense, the difficulties of the GATT negotiations are emblematic of the challenges of the future. (Japan is not the subject of this essay, but a quite similar analysis would apply to that third pole of the "trilateral world." It is not the cohesiveness and insularity of Japanese society that poses the greatest threat to trilateral cooperation, but the fact that Japanese decisionmaking procedures, particularly the emphasis on consensualism rather than strong leadership, gives special blocking powers to veto groups in Japanese politics.)

So far, my argument has been that U.S.-European relations would be enhanced if the leaders on both sides of the Atlantic were less hampered by domestic division and laborious ratification processes. Note, however, that this position presumes that the Atlantic future will be essentially cooperative, for the argument is that the greater the domestic division and the more difficult the ratification process, the less likely that leaders will be able to bring a proposed agreement to fruition. As stated thus far, the argument is essentially symmetrical in that the United States side prefers strong leadership in Europe whereas the European side prefers strong leadership in America.

But if either side expected the other to be fundamentally hostile in the years ahead, then the two-level calculus would be quite different. As I noted earlier, domestic constraints make it more difficult to ratify promises, but they also make it more difficult to ratify threats. A more unified government, less hampered by domestic division or restrictive ratification requirements, finds it easier to deliver on its promises (and is therefore easier to do business with) but also finds it easier to deliver on its threats (and can therefore be more menacing).

From the American point of view, a more integrated Europe would be both a more reliable partner and a more dangerous adversary. (Europeans should feel the same about an America in which the president could count on more reliable congressional support.) If the United States expects a trilateral, cooperative future, it should favor majority voting in the European Council. But if Americans expect a tripolar, conflictful future, they should favor a unanimity rule in European deliberations. The fact that the United States has steadily favored European integration for more than four decades implies that it has expected transatlantic cooperation to be more common than transatlantic conflict. However, if U.S.-European relations threaten to turn sour in some fundamental way, I would expect U.S. policy to switch toward "divide and conquer."

So what is my conclusion about the future of U.S.-European relations? The disappearance of the Soviet threat lowers the threshold for serious conflict over economics and over crises in the Third World. Both Europeans and Americans will need to adjust to a more even sharing of power and responsibility. To deal with this new world of greater equality and greater interdependence, they must together think boldly about how to create new institutional frameworks for collaboration as well as new balances between effective decisionmaking authority and democratic legitimacy. It will require a new era of international institution building, as creative, and farsighted, and bold, and lucky, as the years at the end of World War II when NATO, GATT, the IMF, and so on were created. Yet their shared history of success in bringing freedom, prosperity, and stability to Europe; their shared democratic ideals; and their well-institutionalized habits of cooperation are all important assets on the positive side of the ledger. The challenges and uncertainties are great, but they are no greater than those that Europeans and Americans have faced and surmounted over the past four decades.

NOTES

1. *New York Times,* November 29, 1989, p. A1.

2. John F. Kennedy, *The Burden and the Glory* (New York: Harper & Row 1964), p. 115.

3. Robert D. Putnam, "Diplomacy and Domestic Politics: The Logic of Two-Level Games," *International Organization* 42 (Summer 1988), pp. 427–460.

4. Peter B. Evans, Harold K. Jacobson, and Robert D. Putnam, eds., *International Bargaining and Domestic Politics* (Berkeley: University of California Press, forthcoming).

5. *The Harris Poll,* April 29, 1990.

6. In 1989, U.S. GNP was $5.2 trillion and Spain's GNP was $358 billion, according to *The World Almanac and Book of Facts, 1992* (New York: World Almanac 1991), pp. 802, 815. Assuming a long-term average real growth rate of 3 percent—the actual average during the past decade—U.S. growth over twenty-eight months amounts to $370 billion in 1989 dollars. My point here concerns the size of the American economy as compared to European economies, not a prediction of future growth rates on either side of the Atlantic, although it is worth bearing in mind that over the past two decades America grew slightly faster than Europe. See *OECD Economic Outlook,* no. 48 (December 1990), Table R.1.

7. "Inaugural Address," *New York Times,* January 21, 1989, p. A10.

8. John E. Rielly, ed., *American Public Opinion and U.S. Foreign Policy, 1991* (Chicago: Chicago Council on Foreign Relations 1991).

9. Catherine McArdle Kelleher, Chapter 9 of this volume.

10. *The Polling Report* 6, no. 10 (May 21, 1990), p. D22.

11. Henry R. Nau, "Where Reaganomics Works," *Foreign Policy,* no. 57 (Winter 1984–85), pp. 14–37.

PART TWO

Roles and Policies

6

Patrons and Clients: New Roles in the Post–Cold War Order

Joseph S. Nye, Jr.

The bipolar structure of power that centered around the United States and the Soviet Union seemed stable for nearly half a century. Some political scientists even theorized about the inherent stability of a bipolar world.[1] But social change occurring under the surface led to the East European revolutions in 1989 and the unification of Germany in 1990. Even the events in the Persian Gulf after August 1990 were influenced by the change in the underlying structure of world power. The fears caused by the decline of Iraq's ultimate superpower protector, the Soviet Union, may have contributed to Saddam's hasty and rash action of invading neighboring Kuwait in August 1990.

It is unlikely that all the political tremors are over. The second Russian revolution is still in its early stages, and the fate of the Soviet Union is in question. The decline in Soviet power has been accompanied by the increasing economic integration of Europe and the rise of Japanese economic power. Throughout history, the rapid rise and fall of great powers has created wakes of turmoil. Order is often associated with the stable distribution of power that follows great wars, but order is not the same as justice. The Cold War was associated with order if not justice. Now the bipolar structure of order that followed World War II has broken down and the shape of a new order remains open and fluid.

What will be the shape of the new world order? Some analysts, such as Paul Kennedy in *The Rise and Fall of the Great Powers,* describe the change in the world as the decline of the superpowers, including both the Soviet Union and the United States.[2] In my book *Bound to Lead: The Changing Nature of American Power,*[3] I argue that Kennedy is half right. The United States is not in decline, but the changing nature of power in world politics will require a new relationship between the United States and Europe. In fact, the United States is the only superpower, yet hegemony will be impossible. The United States will be "bound to lead" because of the responsibilities incurred by its large size. If the largest consumer of collective goods does not take a lead in their production, the goods are unlikely to be adequately produced. The United States in a post–Cold War world will be less able to command others than in the past; instead it must assume a role in persuading others to form coalitions and institutions to deal with new problems, problems in interdependence that will require greater use of soft power resources. Whether Americans will have the patience to assemble such coalitions and whether other countries will see a common interest is an open question. In structural terms, the United States will remain the largest state, but there will be diffusion of power and growth of multiple interdependencies.

SOVIET DECLINE
AND THE END OF BIPOLARITY

The Soviet Union ended World War II with the world's largest army and appeared to threaten the security of Europe. Within four years, it had developed nuclear weapons and a decade later ballistic missiles that could threaten the United States. In the 1950s and 1960s Soviet economic growth exceeded 6 percent per year. Not only was the Soviet Union strong in the traditional military and economic measures of hard power, but it was also well endowed in the soft power of cultural and ideological appeal. After World War II, communism was still associated with the resistance to fascism and enjoyed political popularity in many countries. Moreover, the transnational political institutions of Communist parties provided an additional source of soft power for the Soviet Union. When Nikita Khrushchev visited the United States in 1959, his boast that the Soviet Union would bury the United States was taken seriously. The plan to exceed the West capitalist economies by 1980 was written into the program of the Communist party of the Soviet Union. As late as 1976, Leonid Brezhnev told the president of France that communism would dominate the world by 1995.[4] In the American election of 1980, shortly after the Soviet invasion of Afghanistan, some politicians were arguing that the United States had fallen to second place in world power behind the Soviet Union. Yet, at about the same time, a number of Soviet economists and sociologists were beginning to realize that in the 1970s the Soviet Union had begun a process of long-term economic decline.

What were the causes of Soviet decline? Put simply, the Stalinist central planning system was unable to cope with the third industrial revolution. The Stalinist system had been successful in the reconstruction following World War II by forcing peasants off the land and into factories where they made large lumpy goods such as steel and trucks. But by the 1970s the world was experiencing new technological changes. The scarcest resources in modern economies were no longer raw materials or heavy capital goods but information. The ability to use information flexibly and broadly throughout a society became a key source of economic success. The Soviet central planning system was far too cumbersome to allow such flexibility. As a net result, the Soviet Union began to fall further and further behind the capitalist economies of North America, Europe, and Japan, which were pioneering in the third industrial revolution. Not only did the Soviet Union lack the widespread networks of computers married to telecommunications systems, but it also fell behind in the use of microchips in smart machinery. With product cycles shortening to a few years, by the time orders were placed, approved, and filled under the central planning system, the items had often become obsolete.

The Soviet dilemma is illustrated by the fact that when Mikhail Gorbachev came to power in 1985 the Soviet Union had only 50,000 personal computers in the whole country, whereas at that time the United States had some 30 million personal computers.[5] As the Soviet economist Nikolai Schmelov reported, only 8 percent of Soviet industry is of world standard.[6] It is difficult to remain a superpower when 92 percent of industry is below par. As early as 1984, Marshal Ogarkov, then chief of staff, had pointed out that the battlefield of the future would depend upon smart weapons and rely upon an advanced civilian industrial base. At that time, the so-called period of stagnation, he was eased out of office because of his views. But as the Gulf War demonstrated, Ogarkov was correct.

This is not to argue that the Soviet Union (or Russia) will not continue to be a great power. It is still the world's largest oil producer, still has vast natural resources, a large educated population, and of course some 30,000 nuclear weapons. But in the absence of the economic reforms that allow it to enter the information-based age, the Soviet Union will be like a glacier that keeps moving long after the snows have stopped falling. The political problems that accompany the efforts of reform in the Soviet Union may lead to increasing fragmentation and political turmoil. It is impossible to predict the future of the Soviet Union any more than it would have been possible to predict the future of the French Revolution in 1791. Soviet, or Russian, power will remain formidable, but the prospects for the Soviets to retain their status as a global superpower in the next decade seem slight.

AMERICA NOT IN DECLINE

For forty years, American strategy was largely defined by the perception of a Soviet threat. Now Americans are debating their future role in the world. Victory in the Cold War was followed not by a mood of triumphalism but by one of unease. Before the Gulf War, polls showed half the American public believing the country was in decline.[7] A rash of books and articles were published about the decline of nations in general and the position of the United States in particular. "Declinists" see the United States, like previous empires, in a long-term decline. They think the events in the Persian Gulf were only an interruption. "Revivalists" argue that though the country has serious problems, it is still capable of mastering them.

Declinists and revivalists agree that the United States is less powerful now than it was at mid-century. Even conservative estimates show that the U.S. share of global product declined from more than a third of the total in 1950 to a little more than a fifth in the 1980s. However, one must take into account the "World War II effect." Unlike other countries, the United States was strengthened by the war. The relative decline from 1945 to 1975 was simply a return to normal after the artificial effects of World War II. The American share of world product actually held constant at 23 percent after the mid-1970s. The American share of the product of the major industrial democracies actually increased slightly in the 1980s.[8]

In assessing the change in American power, one must also beware of the "golden glow of the past." If one exaggerates the extent to which the United States dominated in the past, one is bound to feel diminished in the present. Even at the peak of its power, the United States was not able to prevent the Soviet Union or France from developing nuclear weapons, nor could it prevent the "loss" of China, Cuba, or Vietnam. The United States was never such an imperial colossus.

Similar problems plague efforts to measure and evaluate the serious social problems in the United States such as drug use, violence, racism, family instability, and the fact that a quarter of the population do not complete secondary school. Some of these problems, such as drug use, are worse today than thirty years ago. Others, such as racism or the position of women in society, are somewhat better than thirty years ago. Still others are hard to evaluate. For example, high school completion rates are higher than thirty years ago, but much lower than Japan's 95 percent, and the performance is inadequate for the needs of an information-based economy. It is clear, however, that if one compares only the bad in the present with the good in the past, it is easy to show decline. Problems have to be dealt with on their own merits.

The United States also has economic problems. Important industrial sectors such as consumer electronics and automobiles have slipped badly. The household savings rate dropped from 8 percent in the 1970s to 5 percent in the late 1980s. In addition, the government's deficit contributed another 3 percent drop in net savings. Because gross investment stayed roughly the same, the missing savings were made up by capital imports that transformed the United States into the world's largest debtor nation in absolute terms. If U.S. savings rates remain low and it becomes more difficult to attract foreign capital in the 1990s, investment rates will suffer with attendant negative effects on productivity and growth.

Again, if one looks only at the negative side of the ledger, the situation seems glum. But there is another side of the story. During the 1980s, the American economy grew by 2.5 percent a year, more than its historical average of 2 percent per annum over the past century. Contrary to the view that the United States is becoming "deindustrialized," manufacturing contributed the same one-fifth of gross national product that it did in the 1970s. Moreover, productivity in manufacturing rose by 3.5 percent per year in the 1980s, and absolute productivity (product per worker) remained higher than in Japan or Germany.[9] In other words, it is a mistake to generalize from autos or consumer electronics to all industry. The United States continues in the forefront of industries such as aircraft, chemicals, biotechnology, and computers. Moreover, some economists believe that the slow 1 percent rate of growth of overall labor productivity (i.e., in all sectors) is an underestimate that reflects the difficulty of measuring productivity increases in the service sector.

In short, the United States has serious domestic problems, particularly improving education and savings that underlie investment and future gains in productivity. In addition, there are serious social problems related to poverty, race, and the condition of inner cities.

Unless these problems are addressed, the future will be diminished. In a world of transnational interdependence, effective international measures start at home. Moreover, the international problems that confront the United States stem not from decline but from the growth of interdependence and the diffusion of power. The United States is more intertwined with the rest of the world. For example, exports and imports combined now represent 21 percent of GNP, which is nearly double the level of twenty years ago.[10]

Some analysts have argued that the United States suffers from "imperial overstretch," the theory that as nations expand their economic interests across borders they develop a political and military structure to defend those interests but that gradually the costs of that structure erode the domestic base of their economy and they go into decline. This theory helps to explain the experience of previous empires like Philip II's Spain and Louis XIV's France, where more than 90 percent of the budgets went to the military.[11] Such theories do not, however, explain the position of the United States where the trends are in the opposite direction from what is predicted by the theory. In the 1950s, at the height of the Cold War, the United States spent 11 percent of its GNP on military. Today it spends less than half of that, and, according to the Bush administration, defense spending is projected to decline to 3.5 percent of GNP by the mid-1990s. In short, the tapering off of the Cold War and the decline of the Soviet Union greatly reduces the burden on the United States and makes the theory of imperial overstretch questionable.

Ironically, in some ways, depending on the uncertain outcome of the "second Russian Revolution," the end of the Cold War could increase American influence with its allies. Because of fear of Soviet power and the spread of communism during the Cold War, Americans often made concessions to their allies. In the post–Cold War period, even though the United States and its allies will have a much lower fear of the Soviet Union (or Russia) than in the earlier period, if American fears are less than those of Europe and Japan (which are proximate to the Soviet Union), then the willingness to make concessions to allies in overall bargaining may also be less. This may not happen, of course, but it does suggest the importance of perceptual as well as structural factors. In structural terms, American power resources declined from a post–World War II artificial high point until 1975. That had clear effects. But the major adjustments to that decline occurred in the early 1970s under the Nixon administration when the Americans finally accepted defeat in Vietnam and when they ended the convertibility of the dollar into gold.

The structural changes in the U.S. position since 1975 have not been as dramatic, but the effects have not been determined purely by structural causes. Even when a country has major power resources, it may not choose to use them. There remains a possibility that the United States might turn inward rather than contribute to world order. For example, in World War I the United States had been a major factor in tipping the balance of military power and emerged as the world's largest economy. Yet during the 1920s and 1930s the United States turned inward and failed to contribute to economic order or collective security on the world scene. The results were the disastrous events of the Great Depression and the spread of fascism in the 1930s, which led to World War II.

AMERICAN STRATEGIC CHOICES

The shape of the post–Cold War world will depend in part on the strategic choices made by the world's largest power. If the United States neglects its alliances, Japanese and European fears will increase. Moreover, as interdependence and the diffusion of power to nonstate actors and small states grow, the implications for stability and welfare will depend heavily on whether the largest state takes a lead in forming coalitions and developing institutions to promote international order.

Not all Americans agree that U.S. leadership is important. Without the galvanizing challenge of a totalitarian threat such as fascism or communism, some observers argue for more investment at home and less abroad. Throughout its history, American foreign policy has been marked by cycles of inward and outward orientation. With 30 percent of its resources going to government, the United States is more lightly taxed than other industrialized countries and can afford both domestic and international security, particularly because the military burdens should be lighter in a post–Cold War world. Some retrenchment from past high levels is still consistent with an international role. But why, many Americans ask, should they still worry about leadership?

The simplest answer is in the new dimensions of interdependence. Drawing back from current international commitments will not stop technological change, or the development and global extension of an information-based economy, or a high degree of dependence upon transnational actors. Terrorism, drug traffic, AIDS, and global warming will intrude upon Americans whether they like it or not. Nor are there purely domestic solutions to such transnational problems.

Absence of leadership by the largest country would reduce the ability of all states to deal with such problems of interdependence. Managing interdependence is a major reason for investing American resources for international leadership and must be central to a new strategy.

There are also traditional geopolitical problems that if ignored could create security problems for the United States. The lessons from earlier periods indicate that if the strongest state does not lead, the prospects for instability increase. The Cold War may be over, but the reduced role of ideology does not mean the end of history, nor does it allow states to be indifferent to the balance of power. In Asia, for example, many conflicts and regional balances have roots that antedate the Cold War and will outlast it. The United States is the only country with both economic and military power resources in the Pacific. Many Asian countries desire a continued American security presence because they do not want Japan to remilitarize. The domestic political consensus in Japan is currently opposed to such a military buildup. The U.S. interest in the stability of the Asian balance, and in obtaining Japanese help on transnational issues, is best served by continuing its alliance and security presence in the region.

The United States has a continuing interest in European security for several reasons. Because Soviet (or Russian) intentions could change, the mere existence of their impressive and proximate military capabilities cannot be ignored. Declining empires have lashed out before. Second, the American security presence, even at greatly reduced troop levels, has a reassuring effect as European integration proceeds. Finally, the situation in Eastern Europe could become politically disruptive as some of those economically weak nations move toward greater national assertiveness. The United States has an interest in a secure and prosperous Western Europe that gradually draws the East European economies and societies toward pluralism and democracy. The primary role will rest with the Europeans, but if the United States were to divorce itself from the process it might find the future geopolitical situation far less stable.

The United States has been strongly supportive of European integration throughout the postwar period. Indeed, early in the postwar period the United States accepted discrimination against American goods for the sake of encouraging a stronger and more integrated Europe because a strong Europe was seen as a bulwark against communism and the encroachment of Soviet power. Economic disputes, of which there have been many going back to the famous chicken war in the 1960s, were generally kept under control because of overarching security concerns. There were many points of consultation between the United States and Europe, and the NATO structure in particular led to a constant and intimate interaction. Now with the Cold War threat removed, NATO plays a somewhat less central role and the European Community has become the dominant institution in Europe. Over the course of the decade, this transition is likely to continue. The United States remains sympathetic and supportive toward European integration, but there have been frequent complaints about European tendencies to resolve internal difficulties among the twelve member states without adequate consultation with the United States and sometimes at the expense of American economic interests.

The American government has suggested a number of times the desirability of better communication between the European Community and the United States but has been resisted on the grounds that the Americans do not deserve the thirteenth seat at the European table. In the meantime, the fact that more issues are dealt with by trade and functional ministries and that fewer of these issues appear on the agendas of top political leaders means that the prospects for friction seem to be increasing. Moreover, even with goodwill, the preoccupation of Europeans with the difficult task of consolidating the unification of Germany, perfecting the community of the twelve, and gradually integrating the outer ring of European neighbors into a viable larger community pushes American concerns to the back burner. This, in turn, fans resentment in Congress, which then tends to revive the issue of burden sharing in the security area as well. The fact that the United States provided such a large share of the troops in the Gulf War is cited by some in Congress as an example of Europeans failing to pay their fair share, although the performance of British, French, and Italian forces, and the increased German financial contribution, somewhat alleviated the problem. Europeans, however, argue that they do not wish to be a tail on an American dog wagged by American conceptions of their interest in the Middle East. They complain that Americans failed to consult with them and then expected them to take part. Americans complain about their allies seeking a free ride, but if Americans want others to pay full freight they will have to be more alert to the problems of discussion and consultation.

The dominant American long-term interest is stability in Europe because twice in this century the United States was drawn into European conflicts under the worst possible circumstances. The best prospects for stability in Europe lie in strengthening the European Community and having it serve as a democratic magnet for countries to its East and as a possible partner for dealing with issues of global interdependence. A stronger Community means increased trade frictions, but the benefits outweigh the costs for American foreign policy. Moreover, because America's ability to attract Europe into coalitions will depend in part on soft, attractive power, efforts to resist European integration would be counterproductive.

ALTERNATIVE VISIONS OF WORLD ORDER

The Cold War order is over, but the shape of a new world order is far from clear. There are at least five major alternative visions of the future—structural settings for the global context of U.S.-European relations.

Return to Bipolarity

Some observers, witnessing the turn to the right in the Soviet Union in winter 1991, argued that the proclamations that the Cold War had ended and bipolarity was over were premature. Either Gorbachev would be replaced or Gorbachev himself would lead a movement to the right. In their view, the Soviet economy was approaching dire circumstances after five years of frenetic reforms that fell short of marketization and decentralization and did nothing to restore the health of the Soviet economy. At the same time that perestroika failed, democratization and glasnost opened a Pandora's box of class and ethnic problems, because when people were allowed to express their wishes it became apparent that the Soviet empire had been held together in part by coercion. Under these circumstances, Gorbachev turned to the structures of the past, that is, the army, the KGB, and the party apparatus, in hopes of preventing the disintegration of the Soviet Union. The skeptics argue that the "new thinking" in foreign policy will not survive a sharp turn to the right and that a harsh climate of international relations will reappear. Given the remaining Soviet military strength, particularly at the nuclear level, this could suggest a return to bipolarity and a little Cold War.

Such an outcome, however, is not plausible for at least two reasons. Internally, even if the movement to the right occurs and the old political structures are used to limit liberalization, a Soviet Union preoccupied with internal dissent and disintegration could as easily turn inward as outward. The old ideological glue of communism and its global mission has been removed and the ideological soft power that the Soviet Union enjoyed in the first decade after

World War II cannot be regained. Second, if the preceding analysis of the causes of Soviet decline is correct, efforts to recentralize the Soviet economy will accelerate rather than reverse the process of decline. After all, if the problem that the Soviets face grows out of their overcentralization and inability to respond flexibly to the information revolution, then returning to a repressive society and a centralized economic planning system will accentuate rather than alleviate the situation that brought about their economic decline in the first place. Thus the prospects for a return to bipolarity seem slight.

Multipolarity

If the future world order will not be fully bipolar, will it be multipolar? Some theorists argue that the flexible shifting of alliances associated with classical multipolar balance of power will be a new source of stability in global politics. However, the development of a true multipolarity of five countries (the United States, the Soviet Union, Europe, China, and Japan) with similar levels of power resources in several categories is not likely to occur in the coming decade. If multipolarity means nothing more than a diffusion of power, then it is already here. But if it refers to a number of roughly equal powers able and willing to shift alliances, such as occurred in the nineteenth century or in the 1930s, it is unlikely to appear. Of the possible contenders for a multipolar position, China remains a less developed country, Europe still lacks unity, and Japan (though impressive in its economic growth) has a limited portfolio of power resources. Given the increased role of Europe and Japan in the economic area, it is plausible to speak of economic multipolarity, but when it comes to the full range of issues in world politics that go into shaping world order, it is hard to see full multipolarity because the United States is the only country with a wide portfolio of power resources.

Three-Bloc or Two-Bloc World

Some observers believe that a declining role of military force, the rise of protectionism, and the uneven growth rates among international economies will give rise to a division of the world into three economic blocs that will eventually shape the structure of world order. This argument sees the United States concentrating on North America and the Western hemisphere; Japan forming the heart of a yen bloc in East Asia; and Europe as the center of a larger, self-sustained European region with Africa as an appendage. Alternatively, tripolar situations often divide two against one. Given Europe's internal preoccupations, the world may divide again into two large blocs, one based in Europe and the other on the Pacific Basin. In fact, Jacques Attali, in his book *Lignes d'Horizon,* argues that the declining United States will ally with a dominant Japan in a Pacific regional bloc that will be opposed to a European bloc to which the Soviet Union will gradually align itself.[12]

Trends in technology and economics run against a bloc view. Some corporations will be satisfied with protected niches, whereas others wishing to achieve economies of scale in global markets will not want to be limited to one-third of the potential market. In that sense, some strong economic and political forces will resist fragmentation of the international economy. Also, the idea of separate blocs runs counter to the nationalism of many of the areas lumped together. For example, Latin Americans do not want to become solely dependent on the United States, Asians do not want to be limited to a yen bloc, and Africans and East Europeans do not want to be mere appendages of Western Europe. For those who are concerned about their neighbors, maintaining an open international economy with access to those outside the region will remain important in the 1990s. In that regard, other parts of the world may develop an interest in international cooperation rather than in separate blocs.

Finally, the three-bloc view runs counter to the fact that even after the Cold War America remains important to the security of both Europe and East Asia. As long as residual concerns remain about the outcome of the second Russian revolution and the potential threat that the Soviet Union (or Russia) can pose to Western Europe, an American security guarantee remains valuable. Similarly, as long as Japan retains its peace constitution in a region where other states, particularly China and the Soviet Union, retain nuclear weapons, an American security guarantee remains an important part of the geopolitical stability of that region. But it is hard to imagine the security guarantees retaining their credibility if the world economy degenerates into trade wars and isolated trading regions. The demand for common security, even if less intense than during the Cold War, may still serve to dampen some of the economic conflicts.

Unipolar Hegemony

Some observers noting the decline of the Soviet Union and the success of the United States in the Gulf War have argued that the world is now witnessing a "unipolar moment."[13] In their view, the United States has emerged as the only superpower and the Americans will be able to dominate world politics over the coming decade. Although the premise of America remaining the only superpower is correct, the hegemonic conclusion does not follow for at least three reasons. First of all, there is little sign of public support for such a role. Second, as argued earlier, the world has become economically multipolar. The United States, Europe, and Japan account for two-thirds of world product today, just as they did twenty years ago, and are likely to do so for some time in the future. Thus economic multipolarity, though not new, does restrict any temptations Americans might have to exercise a hegemonic role.

The third reason that American hegemony is unlikely is the diffusion of power in world politics. Rather than the traditional rise and fall of great powers with its attendant turmoil, the new world order will see a different problem. All the great powers will be less able to use their traditional power resources to achieve their purposes than in the past. On many issues private actors and small states will become more powerful. At least five trends contribute to this diffusion of power: rising economic interdependence, the greater role of transnational actors, the strength of nationalism in otherwise weak states, the spread of technology (including the technology of weaponry), and the increasing number of issues that are both domestic and international. Because most of the resulting issues cannot be managed unilaterally, states will have a strong incentive to develop international cooperation. Rather than exercising power as a hegemon, the United States will need to use its soft power resources to organize coalitions and to persuade others to cooperate in dealing with these new issues relating to the diffusion of power in world politics.

A Multilevel Structure

Traditional accounts of international order see military force as the dominant instrument of power. Although force does remain the ultimate form of power in a self-help system of separate states, it has become more costly for modern great powers to use than in earlier centuries. Other instruments such as communications, organizational and institutional skills, and manipulation of interdependence have become important instruments of power. The less dependent or less vulnerable party in an interdependent relationship may derive power from threats to manipulate that interdependence.[14] Furthermore, interdependence is often balanced differently in different issues, such as security, trade, and finance. Thus creating and resisting linkages between issues when a nation is either less or more vulnerable than the other becomes the art of the power game. Political leaders use international institutions to discourage or promote such linkages.

Traditional accounts of world politics often refer to an international order resulting from a balance of power. Although a balance of military power remains important to a stable world order, different issues have different distributions of power, that is, different power structures. Trade, ocean resources, money, space, shipping, and airlines each have a somewhat different distribution of power. The power of states varies, as does the significance of nonstate actors in different issues.

If military power could be transferred freely across economic and ecological issues, the different levels of structures would not matter and the overall hierarchy determined by military strength would accurately predict outcomes in world politics. But military power is more costly and less transferable today than in earlier times. Thus there is more diversity in the hierarchies that characterize different issues. The games of world politics are being played by different actors with different piles of chips at different tables.[15] They can transfer winnings among tables, but often only at a considerable discount. Military strength and the overall structure of the balance of power determine the world order when survival of states is clearly at stake, but in much of the agenda of modern world politics physical survival is not the most pressing issue. Thus it is best to understand the order of the post–Cold War world as one in which the overall structure of the balance of power will depend heavily on the United States, but that position will not determine the outcomes in what were previously subordinate issues of world politics. The current order might be compared to a layer cake: The Americans predominate in the top military layer, the economic middle layer is multipolar (and has been for two decades), and the bottom layer of transnational interdependence is characterized by a diffusion of power.

INTERNATIONAL INSTITUTIONS
AND SHARING THE BURDENS OF ORDER

In such a world, no one country will be able to create a stable world order. Governments will need to pay more attention to strengthening and developing international institutions. The United States and Europe will both have long-term interests in forming coalitions to deal with such issues, but given the size of the United

States and the internal preoccupation of an integrating Europe, the United States will need to take a lead in establishing coalitions and institutions. In the security area, the United Nations may now play a larger role. For the forty years of the Cold War, the collective security provisions of the United Nations charter were in abeyance, although the organization was often able to play a useful if more modest role with peacekeeping operations meant to prevent conflicts from escalating beyond their regional settings. Iraqi's invasion of Kuwait was remarkable insofar as it was the first instance of UN peacekeeping since the Korean War in 1950. If the United Nations had failed in such a clear-cut case of aggression, collective security would have been a dead letter in the post–Cold War world order.

Nonetheless, it is important to realize some of the limitations of the Persian Gulf case. The United Nations has always been more successful when borders are crossed rather than in civil wars, and Saddam Hussein's proclaimed annexation of Kuwait was a clear challenge to collective security. In the more murky circumstances of domestic conflict and civil war, there is a greater chance that one of the permanent members will veto UN participation. It is also worth noting that when the Gulf crisis went beyond sanctions to military operations, the United States had a preponderant role. One of the questions for the future is whether it would be possible to develop a greater role for a United Nations military staff. Even where the full procedures for collective security cannot be applied, the United Nations may be able to do more in conciliation, peace observation, and peacekeeping than it did during the Cold War.

In addition to security, the international agenda includes ecological dangers, migration, terrorism, and transnational drug trade—examples of the diffusion of power to private nonstate actors in international affairs. Increasingly such issues do not place one state against another; rather they are issues in which all states try to control nonstate transnational actors or private actors within their own and each other's societies. The solutions to many issues of transnational interdependence will require cooperation among governments. Although military force may sometimes play a role, traditional instruments of power are rarely sufficient to deal with the new transnational issues. In some instances, such as ecological threats, it may be possible to organize international agreements by which states will change domestic policies concerning energy or conservation. In other areas, such as drugs, sharing information about drug traffic and reducing demand or working together to confront countries that provide sources of drugs will be important. Sharing information and joining together to isolate countries that provide havens is important to fight terrorism. These cases illustrate how governments are losing some of their ability to control private actors who easily cross national borders. Because unilateral efforts to curtail interdependence often prove costly and ineffective, a new challenge for the 1990s and beyond is more attention to international institutions that coordinate action among governments.

Multilateral institutions help governments in four major ways.

1. They facilitate burden sharing by establishing standards and procedures for consultation.
2. They provide the shared information that is essential for effective action on issues that cross borders.
3. They facilitate diplomacy by giving government officials access to each others' policymaking processes through negotiations and personal contacts, which, in turn, allow them to anticipate more confidently their partners' reactions to hypothetical events.
4. They establish rules and procedures that help reinforce continuity and a long-term focus in contrast to what typically prevails in domestic politics. By representing long-term self-interest, institutions help to provide discipline in the politics of democracies. Institutions help to anchor transnational coalitions and focus larger interests.

For example, during the past half century, the world economy has benefited from international trade that has grown more rapidly than economic production. Part of the credit belongs to technological changes, but part also belongs to the GATT system, which created a transnational coalition in favor of trade. Within each democracy, domestic interests that feel threatened by competition sue for governmental protection from outside influences, but the institutionalized promise of reciprocity in accepting exports of other nations created a countervailing transnational coalition in the domestic politics of the industrial countries. If the GATT system did not exist or were allowed to deteriorate, Europe, the United States, and other countries would be the worse off. Economists have long worried about the provision of collective, or public, goods. A public good is one that, if produced by any member of a group, cannot be withheld from any member of the group. Many members fail to contribute fully because they know they are likely to receive the benefits whether they contribute fully or not. Security is a classic example of this free-rider problem. If one nation provides security, others are tempted to accept it as a gift or to resist paying in full what it might cost. Thus there are always likely to be frictions over burden sharing in the provision of public goods, whether within a country or among a group of countries. During the Cold War, there were constant disputes between the United States and its allies as to whether the allies were doing enough to share the burden of common defense against the Soviet Union.

To some extent, international order is a public good, but different countries may see order in different ways. Given the diffusion of power, weakened perceptions of threats, and the domestic nature of many transnational challenges, it will be more difficult in the 1990s to define common interests and the collective good. Thus to ensure effective cooperation, the United States and Europe must share the processes of defining problems and making decisions. Common institutions and consultations can facilitate these processes.

Because the United States retains preponderant military power, it will be tempted to assert what is the collective good and then demand that others share the burden. But such leadership is less likely to be effective in the post–Cold War order. Other countries may not perceive the situation in the same way and therefore may legitimately resist taking up the burden. Moreover, for some economic issues in international politics, such as maintaining an open trading system, the problem of burden sharing is more than writing checks—it also involves structural adjustments. This is an area where the United States must adjust its attitudes, for though it may be the largest power in the post–Cold War world, no large country will be able to achieve what it wants unilaterally. If the United States wants Europeans and others to join coalitions and share the burden of maintaining an accepted world order, it will have to use multilateral institutions to develop the habit of decision sharing. If others pay, they will have a right to say. Another way of putting it is that although some Europeans were free riders, the Americans had full control of the steering wheel. If Europeans pay a full fare, they will have a greater say about where the bus will go. Thus there will be no easy answers to the challenges of world order in the post–Cold War world, and we are only beginning to see how the dynamics of interaction between the three layers of the system will be worked out.

NOTES

1. Kenneth Waltz, *Theory of International Politics* (Reading, Mass.: Addison-Wesley 1979).

2. Paul Kennedy, *The Rise and Fall of the Great Powers: Economic Change and Military Conflict from 1500 to 2000* (New York: Random House 1987).

3. Joseph S. Nye, Jr., *Bound to Lead: The Changing Nature of American Power* (New York: Basic Books 1990).

4. *Wall Street Journal,* February 6, 1989.

5. *New York Times,* May 30, 1988.

6. Nikolai Schmelov, "Advances and Debts," *Novy Mir,* June 1987, p. 12.

7. *New York Times,* February 23, 1989; also John E. Rielly, ed., *American Public Opinion and U.S. Foreign Policy, 1991* (Chicago: Chicago Council on Foreign Relations 1991). Just before the Gulf War, 35 percent of the public believed that the United States played a less important role in the world and 37 percent said that it played a more important role. In the early post-Vietnam period, the balance said that the United States played a less important role. In 1986, only 26 percent said that the United States played a less important role.

8. For details, see Nye, *Bound to Lead.*

9. *New York Times,* February 5, 1991.

10. U.S. Department of Commerce, Bureau of the Census, *Statistical Abstract of the United States, 1988* (Washington, D.C.: Government Printing Office 1987), p. 425.

11. Kennedy, *Rise and Fall of the Great Powers.*

12. Jacques Attali, *Lignes d'Horizon* (Paris: Fayarde 1990).

13. Charles Krauthammer, "The Unipolar Moment," *Foreign Affairs* 70, no. 1 (1990/91), pp. 23–33.

14. Robert O. Keohane and Joseph S. Nye, Jr., *Power and Interdependence* (Boston: Little, Brown 1977).

15. See Robert D. Putnam, Chapter 5 of this volume.

7

Regions in Competition: Comparative Advantages of America, Europe, and Asia

Peter J. Katzenstein

Recent events in world politics are creating a substantial break in the history of international politics comparable in this century only to the years from 1917 to 1922 and 1947 to 1953. The most important causes for this break were changes inside the Soviet Union and the strategic retreat that the Soviet leadership under Gorbachev initiated abroad and at home. The political revolution in Central and Eastern Europe, accompanied by the withdrawal of Soviet troops, would not have been possible without the political reform and economic collapse inside the Soviet Union. Nor would Germany's rapid unification in 1990 have been possible.

But the strategic retreat of the Soviet Union also had a profound effect on the Middle East and Asia. In removing the international restraints acting on Saddam Hussein it contributed to the miscalculations that led to Iraq's invasion of Kuwait in August 1990 and to the formation of the American-led multinational military alliance that defeated Iraq and forced its withdrawal from Kuwait in February 1991. The Gulf War was a boost to American self-confidence. But it was a profound shock to Japan, which went through an agonizing and inconclusive domestic debate on whether the participation in international peacekeeping operations was compatible with its constitution. With the sending of minesweepers in spring 1991 it appears probable that changes in Japan's public opinion will make it possible for future Japanese governments to take a more cooperative stance in international peacekeeping operations.

In regard to balance, recent changes in international politics have helped to pacify several regional conflicts that were inflamed or sustained by the Cold War. The political reorganization of Central Europe and the magnetic appeal that the European integration process has for the new democracies emerging from Communist rule are telling examples. Europe promises the economic assistance, market access, and political legitimacy that offers hope for avoiding the trap of unrestrained ethnic conflicts, Yugoslavia-style, which would move Central Europe back to the late nineteenth century rather than forward into the twenty-first. In Asia, political settlements of conflicts in Cambodia, on the Korean peninsula, and between the Soviet Union and Japan over the northern territories are becoming realistic possibilities. The end of apartheid in South Africa and the end of the long civil war in Ethiopia point to important political changes, as does the ascendance of democratic regimes in many African states in the past two years. The political situation in the Middle East remains unsettled, but the end of the civil war in Lebanon is an occasion for some hope. With electoral defeat of the Sandinistas in Nicaragua and the weakening position of Castro's Cuba, even Central America may possibly be affected by the change in international politics.

In this chapter I argue that underlying these changes in world politics is a new form of political regionalism that will supplement rather than replace the system of military bipolarity that has shaped international politics since the late 1940s, provided that the Soviet Union does not break apart.

AMERICAN REFLECTIONS

The American discussion about the newly emerging international order does not focus on the new regionalism in the world. It concentrates instead on changes in America's political position. The discussion is typically cast in the terms of political realism, still the most important analytical perspective in American analyses of international politics. Two arguments captured the public imagination in 1987 and 1988 and became identified with extreme positions that were quickly dismissed. In Paul Kennedy's historical tome on the rise and fall of great powers,[1] he argued that like all other great powers America was destined to lose its position of international preeminence and that it could only affect the speed of the process of decline. The tendency to live off borrowed money, brought about by the Reagan administration, had all the symptoms of "imperial overstretch," which, left uncorrected, would quickly drive the United States from its international position of power. Francis Fukuyama's slender essay "The End of History"[2] concluded to the contrary that America had prevailed in the great ideological conflict of the twentieth century and that with that great victory came a certain moral staleness and a turning away from great national tasks.

Kennedy's and Fukuyama's critics wasted no time to point out that structural tendencies toward decline are influenced by different policy choices that Kennedy had left unexamined and that the reassertion of ethnic conflicts in the Soviet Union as well as Eastern and Central Europe meant an awakening of history, not its end.

The modified political realism of Henry Nau and Joseph Nye[3] represent a centrist position that is not as easily assailed as are Kennedy's and Fukuyama's bold claims. Their books differ in important ways, both politically and intellectually. Nau is a moderate conservative who was a staff member of the National Security Council in the first Reagan administration. In the interest of stable economic growth at home and abroad as an essential prerequisite for a peaceful international order conducive to the spread of democracy, Nau favors a unilateral American approach to important international problems. Nye is a moderate liberal who served in the Carter administration and had close links with the Mondale and Dukakis campaigns in 1984 and 1988. In the interest of strengthening the role of international institutions that embody many of America's values and interests, Nye favors multilateral diplomacy. International institutions will provide a more secure basis for a peaceful and just evolution of the international order than would American national institutions.

Neither Nau nor Nye is a strict "neorealist." They do not adhere to the value of analytical parsimony that is central to Ken Waltz's basic formulation or John Mearsheimer's controversial application to recent political developments in Europe.[4] For Nau and Nye foreign policy choices are not, as the neorealists insist, simply determined by the distribution of international capabilities. What matters for Nau as well is the influence that ideas play in the process of making policy choices. And Nye stresses the importance of values as well as structures of technological, economic, and social interdependence that leave an indelible imprint on national policy choices.

For Nau, America's national policy in the 1980s has been affected deeply by the economic values that informed the Reagan revolution: an affirmation of private initiative, vigorous investment, stable growth and increasing productivity, and thus a return to the golden 1950s. However, Nau's analysis overlooks the structure of American domestic politics—the political and economic immobilism that has resulted from the permanent conflict between the executive and legislative branches of government. Policy choices of fundamental consequence for the international political economy—energy policy in the 1970s and fiscal policy in the 1980s—have been stymied by this defining characteristic of American politics.

Nye argues that the zone for "hard" power politics has narrowed in world politics. Structures of interdependence have grown and so has the role of "soft" power, the universal appeal of American liberal values. Granting the importance of interdependence structures and English as the only universal language, Nye's analysis of "soft" power is too brief to capture the element of anti-Americanism that is deeply rooted in the global ascendance of liberal values. It is true that the products of American mass culture are admired globally and that America's multicultural society is for many a deeply appealing model in a more pluralist world. But the frequent assertion of America's military power and the economic inefficiencies and social injustices of the American version of capitalism are a source of widespread criticism, not admiration, in Europe, Asia, and throughout the Third World. America is a powerful symbol, as Secretary of State Baker (or "Becker," as one of the posters in the crowd read) experienced during his triumphant eight-hour visit to Albania in summer 1991. But familiarity also breeds contempt or at least lack of comprehension. And Albanians probably have less experience with and knowledge of the United States than almost any other people in the world.

Nau and Nye express the center of the spectrum of American opinion on the current transformation of world politics. But their books focus too much on the resurgence and transformation of American power. They neglect altogether the growing regional pluralism that is characterizing world politics. I argue that regional pluralism expresses the institutionalization of social and political state systems and the normative contexts in which decisionmakers define national interests. Furthermore, regionalism may have important implications for international politics and for American foreign policy.

STRUCTURES AND ACTORS
IN INTERNATIONAL POLITICS

The main protagonists of the Cold War, the United States and the Soviet Union, both lost that war to two trading and welfare states, Japan and Germany, who had learned similar lessons from their disastrous involvement in power politics in the first half of the twentieth century.

The power shift from the United States to Asia, specifically Japan, is a very prominent trend in the 1980s. It can be traced along many dimensions relevant to economic competitiveness and regional political power. Most dramatic and probably most important is the shift in global capital markets. In the history of capitalism there has never occurred a comparable shift of capital in as short a time. The United States moved from a position of creditor of about $350 billion in 1980 to a position of debtor of about $350 billion in 1990. This $700 billion turnaround is reflected in the size of private banks. In the second half of the 1980s, the largest ten banks worldwide were usually Japanese. Tokyo became the richest capital market in the world, which defined the daily mood for trading on Wall Street—a development unthinkable at the beginning of the 1980s. And judging by the inroads that Japanese banks are making in California's financial markets, Japan's newly found financial muscle will have a deep effect on America as well as on the rest of the world.

Japan's technological dynamism, furthermore, is heralding a fundamental shift in political and military relations in coming decades. In the 1980s civilian technologies have come to drive military technologies, an unforeseen development that was appreciated fully by Japanese bureaucrats only when American defense officials became increasingly insistent on having access to some of Japan's civilian technologies with potential military applications. The "spin-on" from commercial to military products is beginning to replace the "spin-off" from military to commercial products. In areas such as electronics, infrared sensors and optics, avionics, new materials, and ceramics, Japan's leading manufacturers are often well ahead of American defense corporations. And Japanese firms enjoy a substantial lead across the board in virtually all aspects of production technologies relevant for the defense industry. The Department of Defense has been aware of this development since the early 1980s.[5] Even though only a few voices anticipate that Japan would wish to exercise direct political power over the United States,[6] the indirect use of Japan's growing commercial-military power is another matter altogether. And even though the American public was mesmerized by the success of America's high-tech weapons in the Gulf War in 1991, specialists know that the victory was won with weapons that embodied the technologies of the mid to late 1970s. Military products have a life cycle of ten to twenty years; commercial products embody new technologies every three to five years, or three times faster. Japanese military officers watching the war on Cable News Network (CNN) must have been very much aware that the restraints on Japan's military power are primarily political, not technological.

Finally, as a prosperous and successful trading state, Japan has developed a deep confidence in the efficacy of markets. It thus took a very different attitude toward Iraq's invasion of Kuwait than did the United States. Because of the energy efficiencies that it has built into its economy since the oil shock of 1973, any increase in the price of oil will enhance rather than diminish its competitiveness over Europe and, in particular, the United States. From Japan's perspective, Saddam Hussein would have had to sell Iraq's and Kuwait's oil eventually. And because Japan could afford to pay for the oil at almost any price, it preferred a diplomatic over a military solution to the Gulf conflict, unlike the Bush administration. Even an Iraqi assault on Saudi Arabia would not have altered the economic logic of Japanese calculations. The objective of protecting a friendly leadership of the Organization of Petroleum Exporting Countries (OPEC) did not figure heavily in Japanese calculations, as it did for the United States. And Japan conspicuously lacked the ideological and political instincts that guided American diplomacy in the Mideast after August 2, 1990. However, when war turned out to be unavoidable, Japan joined Saudi Arabia and Germany as America's most generous financial supporters.

In the foreseeable future there appear to be two limits to Japan's increasing power. First, Japan's political imagination is still too constricted to have developed a clear-cut view of its role in global politics. The criticisms levied against Japan in the wake of the Gulf War and anticipation of the substantial political changes that the end of the Cold War might bring about in Asia are providing a strong impetus for Japan's political leadership to remedy that shortcoming. But it is not clear whether the blueprints that undoubtedly will be generated in the coming months and years will transform Japan's cautious, follow-the-leader approach to diplomacy. It is, for example, widely acknowledged that a thorough modernization of American-owned manufacturing industries is essential for a long-term, stable political relationship with the United States, and in particular the U.S. Congress. Yet Japan's political leadership has made no concerted efforts to address let alone deal with this problem. Instead, the investment strategy of Japanese corporations in Europe points to a magnification of Japan's political troubles in the industrial world in the coming years.

Second, political constraints, both domestic and international, militate against a dramatic rise in Japan's military power. Some shrill voices (magnified by American publishers with a good instinct for what it takes to sell books in Tokyo) talk of "the coming war with Japan."[7] But hardly anyone in Asia or the United States takes such talk seriously at this time. The real change since the late 1970s is rather a gradual military buildup that is creating technological options for a national strategy that did not exist ten or twenty years ago. But as long as Japan is not developing intercontinental ballistic missiles, stealth technologies, and offensive conventional military power in Asia on a large scale, we can be reasonably certain that Japan will operate within the political limits that it has imposed on its exercise of military power since 1945. This is hardly a surprise. Japanese policymakers define national security in comprehensive terms, to include economic, social, and political issues besides military considerations. They are thus much more attuned to finding an appropriate political role for Japan rather than seeking to develop national military options in a world marked by decreasing international tensions. Playing a central, perhaps *the* central, role in an Asia that is defined so broadly to encompass also the United States is a far more urgent and appealing task.

The decline of the Soviet Union and the ascent of Germany have also been very marked trends that found their visible expression in the opening of the Berlin Wall in 1989, German unification in 1990, and the promise of the withdrawal of the last Soviet soldier from German territory by 1994. Several examples illustrate the drastic divergence in the political fortunes of the Soviet Union and Germany. German unification within the context of an integrating Europe and the Western alliance is a culmination of West Germany's foreign policy objectives as articulated by Chancellor Konrad Adenauer in the early years of the history of the Federal Republic. This contrasts with the growing problem of national cohesion that marks the Soviet Union. Besides the three Baltic states, Georgia, Armenia, and Moldavia have refused to join the other nine republics in signing in 1991 the new union treaty. And ethnic tensions are also very evident inside the Communist party and the Soviet army, the last institutional pillars of a centralized Soviet Union. It remains to be seen whether the Soviet Union will survive this period of retrenchment and reform as a decentralized state, whether it will move to a confederate or commonwealthlike structure, or whether it will in fact break apart into a number of different sovereign states.

In economic terms as well, the difference between Germany and the Soviet Union is striking. In winter 1990–1991 Germans organized an unprecedented and spontaneous massive private economic assistance program to help stave off hunger and starvation in the major

Soviet cities where food supplies were reported to be barely adequate. This assistance supplemented extensive credits of the German government, running into tens of billions of dollars over the next several years. Furthermore, Germany has become the most ardent advocate of the Soviet cause; in international meetings Germany has tried to persuade the United States and Japan, which are much less ready to develop a broadly based international economic assistance program, to help revitalize the Soviet economy.

The contrast between the economic crisis in the Soviet Union and that in East Germany underlines the great difference between the two countries. Germany is rich enough to have mobilized in 1991 and 1992 alone more capital for the reconstruction of East Germany than did the United States with the Marshall Plan for the reconstruction of all of Western Europe after World War II. The German economy will turn inward for a few years to repair some of the material damages that forty years of socialism have wrought. But few doubt that it will emerge from this period as a major, if not *the* major, export economy in the global economy.

Finally, the contrast between the Soviet Union and Germany is striking in terms of the model they provide for other states in Central and Eastern Europe. The Soviet Union in 1945 not only offered a political vision to many Europeans but also had a transnational political structure, the Communist party, through which it could affect political developments in most major European states. Forty years later the failure of the Soviet model and that of its former satellites in Central and Eastern Europe has been so dramatic that in the foreseeable future no political leadership can hope to gain or retain positions of power under a program dedicated to building "socialism in one country." The dissolution of the Council for Mutual Economic Assistance (COMECON) and the Warsaw Pact in 1991 symbolize the political exhaustion of the Soviet model.

In contrast, Germany's social market economy is inspiring political confidence in Central Europe as a form of capitalism worth emulating. Economic efficiency, private affluence, and good public services in a political economy that is fully integrated into a larger Europe both economically and politically—these are the targets of economic and political reform efforts throughout Central and Eastern Europe, particularly if the reform and modernization of East Germany succeeds within the next five to ten years. The desire of the governments in Central Europe to become associate members of the EC as quickly as possible expresses both the lack of political alternatives in the East as well as their confidence in the political models of the West, particularly that of Germany.

As is true of Japan, Germany's political role in world politics will remain restricted in the coming years for two reasons. The end of the Cold War as well as the Gulf War showed deep fissures in Germany's political culture. There is no consensus about the role that Germany should play in the world. The mix between political, economic, and military dimensions of power as well as the balance between national initiatives and international obligations remains very much contested. Second, like Japan, Germany is unlikely to emerge as a major independent military power in the near future. German unification brought about a 50 percent cut in the combined military strength of West and East Germany. The German army is an integral part of NATO. In terms of men and equipment, the Soviet forces outnumber Germany's by a ratio of about 10:1. Furthermore, contrary to the claims of some who see Germany producing a national nuclear force to protect itself against ethnic strife in Eastern Europe and in the Soviet Union, a growth in Germany's nuclear military power is highly unlikely under national auspices.[8] Only an integration of Europe's defense policy might make Germany conceivably part of a European deterrent force. Rather than moving back to the politics of 1912, European integration as it is reflected in the EC 92 process offers Germany the chance to participate in a European regional process that will help to define its role in the world in the next century.

THE NORMATIVE CONTEXT
FOR NATIONAL INTERESTS

Because of their historical experiences, the main protagonists and losers of the Cold War, the United States and the Soviet Union, have defined state security largely in military terms. For the United States the trauma of the Japanese surprise attack on Pearl Harbor on December 7, 1941, was perhaps even greater than was the shock in the Soviet Union when German armies began a large-scale invasion under the code word "Barbarossa" on June 22, 1941. The rise of the American air force and the search for absolute protection against the recurrence of a surprise attack, from the "flying fortresses" of the 1950s to President Reagan's program for a Strategic Defense Initiative in the 1980s, are the legacy of a crucial American historical experience. Through superior technology and the system of nuclear deterrence, it was hoped, one could deter surprise enemy attacks. Similarly, the buildup of the Soviet army with its 50,000 tanks (a convoy that reportedly would stretch from Detroit to Seattle if arrayed along one road) and millions of soldiers deployed for forty years to wage offensive war against West Germany and the rest of Europe can be understood fully only as part of the Soviet Union's historical experience in World War II. Having suffered 20 to 30 million casualties in a war that Germany started, preparation for waging an offensive war appeared to be the best way for minimizing suffering for the Soviet population. The Cold War, that is, was not simply born out of the geostrategic realities that, after the defeat of Germany and Japan, left the United States and the Soviet Union as the only two global powers cut loose from their isolationist and autarchic moorings. The Cold War also embodied the historical lesson that these two states learned during the hot war that preceded it: State security could be defended only through military means.

The vanquished learned other lessons than the victors. Germany's and Japan's definition of security de-emphasizes military aspects. The military quest for regional hegemony in Europe and Asia had turned out so disastrously for them that repetition of the attempt to gain military preeminence in the era of nuclear deterrence was an invitation to national suicide. Instead, both states emphasized what the Japanese eventually called "comprehensive security"—a combination of political, military, and economic means for achieving security objectives that could no longer be guaranteed by national military means. The prospect of war, even a war fought by an international coalition with the backing of the United Nations, creates confusion and dissension in these two states, as the Gulf War illustrated, in contrast to the self-confident assertion of American, British, and French military power. The experience of the German and Japanese warfare state before 1945 was so disastrous and that of the German and Japanese trading state after 1945 so successful that contaminating the second with elements of the first cuts very much against the political grain in either country.

But German and Japanese definitions of security interests reflect a different balance of political, military, and economic considerations. Adenauer's policy of rearmament and his entire Western policy, for example, was foremost a political gambit to use West Germany's military potential as a bargaining chip to regain West German sovereignty and to assure for the defense of the Federal Republic the military capabilities of the entire NATO. The formation of the European Community, after the failure of the European Defense Community (EDC), was a political backstop that the West German government supported wholeheartedly because it promised to cement Franco-German relations and thus peace in Europe. With conditions changing both between the two superpowers and within

Europe, West Germany was the leading proponent of the Harmel Report of 1967, which recommended that NATO retain its character as a defensive military alliance with an integrated peacetime command. But the Harmel Report stressed also that NATO should assume the role of an instrument of détente policy. Until Secretary Baker conceded in his Berlin speech in December 1989 that NATO's role was substantially political, this point had remained a source of muted conflict between the United States and Germany. But the Harmel Report provided the basis for Chancellor Willy Brandt's Eastern policy, which was successful in normalizing political relations between West Germany, the Soviet Union, and the states in Eastern Europe. The Conference on Security and Cooperation in Europe (CSCE), which ratified the process of German unification in November 1990, is an institutional legacy of this West German political initiative that, according to German plans, will hopefully provide in the coming years one forum among several in which a pan-European peace order can evolve.

Economic considerations, though important, were secondary. They were largely satisfied by the political integration of the Western community under American leadership. The Bretton Woods system, it turned out, was tailor-made for a West German economy that, after Germany's division, was dependent on export markets in a way in which no previous German regime had been. Without its traditional breadbasket in East Germany and cut off by the Cold War from its traditional markets in the East, West German business and labor cooperated in following a strategy of export-led growth, primarily in European but also in global markets. Trade did not follow the national flag, but it did follow the institutions that the United States had created for a liberalizing international economy. The EC became an increasingly important market in that economy. And once West Germany's economy had been reconstructed, the Federal Republic became a consistently strong voice inside the EC for free trade. But economic considerations were not the driving force behind the main lines of German foreign policy during the past forty years.

The vision that informs Germany's political definition of security is grounded in what could be called an ideology of "security partnership" in an international community of nations. Ordinary language is a good indicator of a great change in German thinking. Before 1945 the concept of "community" was largely coupled with the adjective "national." References to international "society" took a variety of forms, most of which lacked communal connotations. After 1945 West Germans would respond to the term "national community" with about the same enthusiasm as to the name "Adolf." As democratic institutions and practices took hold, domestic affairs were talked and thought of increasingly in terms of "civil society." But West Germany belonged to the Western or Atlantic "community" and of course to the European "community." To conceive of the system of states in terms of security partnerships embedded in an international community is in agreement with the West German experience of a system of "social partnerships" that has regularized conflict between business, unions, and other major interest groups. The precise meaning of a "security partnership" in the international context is never unambiguous. In the current European climate, to the left wing of the SPD (Social Democratic Party) it means the building of a European peace order focused on the needs and interests of Central Europe and the Soviet Union; for the political center in all of the major parties it connotes the acceleration of the European integration process linked to both the continuation of strong ties with the United States and other OECD states as well as the forging of strong connections with the Soviet Union and the Central European states; and for parts of the right wing of the CDU/CSU (Christian Democratic Union/Christian Social Union) it expresses an unwillingness to see any erosion in the Atlantic Community. But common to all of these political conceptions is the readiness to integrate Germany into a variety of international partnerships.

In the case of Japan, economic considerations reigned supreme until the early 1970s, at the expense of virtually all military and political considerations. Prime Minister Yoshida Shigeru resisted the American effort to have Japan participate actively in a regional defense of Asia. Stationed in the vicinity of Japan's major metropolitan areas, the Japanese Self-Defense Forces assumed an indirect policing role instead that was aimed primarily at deterring domestic insurrections. The foreign policy of a strict separation between economic and security issues informed also the policies of Yoshida's two most ardent and successful disciples. After a deeply divisive domestic debate over the renegotiation of the Mutual Security Treaty with the United States in 1960, Prime Minister Ikeda Hayato (1960–1964) succeeded in uniting the nation around his plan to double the national income. Prime Minister Sato Eisaku (1964–1972) continued that growth policy and earned a Nobel Peace Prize for adopting in 1967 the three nonnuclear principles. And as late as the mid-1970s Prime Minister Takeo Fukuda often invoked Japan's omnidirectional, peaceful foreign policy. Only in the 1980s has Japan's foreign policy acquired a distinct security component that has linked

Japan unambiguously to the United States in the role of a junior partner who is fully integrated into the American military, especially the U.S. Navy.

The reconstruction of Japan created an economic dynamism that spilled over into Japan's striking success in export markets, first in the United States and later worldwide. The story of economic success marred by political, that is, protectionist, backlash abroad has become repetitive. Voluntary export restraints in textiles negotiated between the United States and Japan in the mid-1950s eventually were transformed into the Short-Term, Long-Term, and Multi-Fiber agreements that have regulated international markets for textiles and garments since the early 1960s. Voluntary export restraints in steel, negotiated between the United States and Japan in the late 1960s after a brief return to market competition, were replaced by the Trigger Price Mechanism (TPM) in 1978 and soon thereafter by a restrictive, worldwide trade regime in steel. The success of Japan's consumer electronics industry also led to a variety of trade restraints in those export markets. The rise of the Japanese automobile industry caused the imposition of voluntary Japanese restrictions on auto exports after 1981. These became largely superfluous in the late 1980s because Japanese producers had invested so heavily in the U.S. automobile industry that they had become one of the "three big American producers" by the early 1990s. The semiconductor agreement of 1986, which was renewed in 1991, is the latest example of Japanese economic success and international political backlash.

Japan's response to the political consequences of its economic success in international markets has been remarkably consistent. Political bargaining and compromises about some set of "voluntary" limitations have typically followed on the heels of economic success. Most of the time these political agreements were negotiated between Japanese and American officials. Japanese officials have made no sustained political attempts during the past two decades to devise international political solutions to the disturbances that Japan's export offensive was creating in the markets of other capitalist states. Instead, Japan engaged in tough, ad hoc, and, in the end, normally pragmatic bargaining with its trading partners.

The Japanese approach contributed to the gradual erosion of the traditional most favored nation norm, with its open-ended reciprocity over long periods of time, and the emergence of a new "reciprocity" norm that makes international trade dependent on symmetrical market openings over shorter time periods. For a variety of reasons that are typically no longer related to government policy, Japan's markets are less open than those of its major com-

petitors. The new, evolving norm is thus probably not in Japan's
interest. At least this can be inferred from the fact that the Japanese
government has now become an outspoken champion of liberal rules
in international markets. This is true even for markets of raw materials, such as oil, that are critical for the operation of Japan's
industries. Economic efficiency and competitiveness have translated
into financial and market powers sufficiently large to secure for
Japan the necessary raw materials through market transactions
rather than state-to-state bargaining. Japan's economic success, that
is, has had a dramatic effect on its traditional postwar role as a
mercantilist trading state.

Like Germany, Japan's approach to the international system expresses also a basic vision. Japan's vision of security is economic. It
is grounded in a notion of economic partnerships in an international
society of states. According to this view, what holds the world
together are not common norms that tie different nations together
in common endeavors. Instead the world is governed by interests.
International cooperation is made possible by flexibility in the definition of self-interests, in particular the flexibility of redefining
short-term into long-term interests. This ability to redefine interests
presupposes a willingness to extend the notion of "self" to incorporate at least some relevant portions of the "other" so that the expec-
tation of an ongoing interest-based relationship is met.[9] This
approach differs dramatically from the purely market-based American approach, which takes the identity of an autonomous actor's
self as a given. And it differs also from the German and European
experience, which is increasingly putting to question the very nature
of the national self. More concretely, Japan has viewed virtually all
facets of international life in terms of its interest, that is, the effect
that their behavior policies would have on the U.S.-Japanese relationship. Compared to Germany, Japan is both more and less ready
to integrate with other countries. With respect to the United States,
Japan has accepted a condition of vulnerability in economic and
security matters that far exceeds that of the Federal Republic. Yet
Japan has not had the experience of integrating with numerous
Asian countries in different international institutions, which has
been a politically defining experience for Germany in Europe during
the past forty years.

Germany's primarily political and Japan's primarily economic
definitions of security in the postwar world have, however, shared
one common feature, which has tied both of them to the military
definition of security of the two superpowers. Germany in the 1950s
and Japan in the 1980s chose a buildup of their national military

capabilities for political reasons. Germany wanted to regain a standing in the Western community of nations and secure America's nuclear deterrent for its national defense. Japan was intent on cementing its relationship with the United States, which had become increasingly frayed by the recurrence of economic tensions between the two countries. But throughout the postwar years both Germany and Japan benefited greatly from the extension of America's nuclear umbrella over their territories: It permitted them to spend less on national defense than they would have otherwise. The nuclear guarantee posed the risk of Germany or Japan being drawn into a conflict not germane to German or Japanese security. But in the judgment of successive German and Japanese governments, the risk was small compared to the economic and political benefits of a close relationship with the United States. In other words, as was true of the economic institutions of the Bretton Woods system, the nuclear guarantee of the United States offered considerable benefits, which Germany and Japan as the two victors of the Cold War exploited to the best of their abilities. Historical memory and learning made Germany and Japan define their security interests not in narrow military but in broader political and economic terms. But it did not prevent them from seeking the benefits that could be derived from participating indirectly in the system of nuclear deterrence.

NEW REGIONALISM
IN INTERNATIONAL POLITICS

Germany and Japan are the centers of a new regionalism in Europe and Asia that will increasingly complement the system of strategic bipolarity—as long as the Soviet Union does not break apart, Europe does not unite militarily, and Japan forgoes the technological options it has for becoming a military superpower. This regionalism differs from Hitler's New Order and Japan's Co-Prosperity Sphere in the 1930s and 1940s as well as from George Orwell's nightmarish projection of a tripolar world in 1984.[10] What separates the new from the old regionalism is the difference between autarky and direct rule on the one hand and interdependence and indirect rule on the other.

Japan's growing role in the six member states of the Association of Southeast Asian Nations (ASEAN; Indonesia, Thailand, Malaysia, the Philippines, Singapore, and Brunei) can be easily traced in the areas of trade, aid, investment, and technology transfer. In the two decades preceding the Plaza Accord of 1985, Japan accounted for close to half of the total aid and direct foreign investment that the region received. The dramatic appreciation of the yen after 1985 led to a veritable explosion of Japanese investment, which between 1985 and 1989 was twice as large as between 1951 and 1984. And the flow of aid has continued to increase as Japan seeks to recycle its trade surplus with the region. All governments in Southeast Asia are bidding for Japanese capital, as is illustrated by the massive deregulation of their economies as well as the lucrative incentives that they are willing to grant to foreign investors. More important, Japan's "developmental state" has become a model of emulation in both the public and private sector. The establishment of private trading companies and a general commitment of governments in the region to vigorous policies of export promotion give testimony to the widespread appeal of the Japanese model.

The massive inflow of Japanese investments in recent years has created severe bottlenecks in the public-sector infrastructures of countries like Indonesia and Thailand. And these bottlenecks are turning out to be a serious impediment for the future growth of Japanese investment. Roads and ports are insufficient and need to be expanded and modernized. The same is true of national systems of communications and the public services more generally. The New AID Plan (New Asian Industries Development Plan), which Japan revealed in 1987, signals that Japan has serious, long-term interests in the region. The plan addresses the needs of the public sector as they relate to Japanese industrial investments, and the restructuring of the Japanese economy more generally. In broad terms, the program offers investment incentives for select Japanese industries to relocate to ASEAN countries. A large number of Japanese government agencies are cooperating in this plan, which makes explicit Japan's hierarchical view of the international division of labor in Southeast Asia.

To some extent this is also true of Japan's view of its relations with the newly industrialized countries (NICs) of Northeast Asia: South Korea, Taiwan, Hong Kong, and Singapore.[11] These countries' takeoff into self-sustaining rapid growth occurred earlier than in Southeast Asia. In several of these countries, Japanese trade, aid, investment, and technology transfer have been crucial for the rapid success that they have enjoyed in international markets. And Japan proved to be an important model for several of these states as well.

Greater Asian regional cooperation appears to be an idea whose time has come—at least in terms of public debate. Enhanced regional cooperation is often invoked as a necessary response to the process of European integration as well as the Canada-U.S. Free Trade Agreement, which is soon to be joined by Mexico. Demands for an Asian equivalent of the European CSCE subsided after it became clear that for the time being the CSCE was playing no more than a subordinate role in Europe. However, the Asia Pacific Economic Cooperation Conference (APEC) held its first meeting in Canberra in December 1989. Like the Asian Development Bank, it is a forum for the discussion of economic policy and thus may turn out to be useful for strengthening regional economic cooperation.

The sharp growth in Japanese influence and power in Asia has created widespread unease about the political consequences of intensifying economic relations for an emerging regional political economy. Japan's power is simply too large to be met in the foreseeable future by any coalition of Asian states. With the total GNP of ASEAN amounting to no more than about 15 percent of Japan's GNP, a world of self-contained regions in the northern half of the globe would leave the ASEAN members at the mercy of a Japanese colossus. In the view of the other Asian countries only the United States can act as an indispensable counterweight to Japan's growing power.

With the American navy firmly committed to retaining a strong position in Asia and with the consolidation of U.S.-Japanese security arrangements in the 1980s, the United States is likely to remain an Asian power. Furthermore, because virtually all Asian countries run a substantial trade deficit with Japan and a large surplus with the United States, the United States is essential for regional economic integration in Asia. An Asia that includes the United States has several virtues. It can diffuse the economic and political dependencies of the smaller Asian states away from Japan. And it can provide Japan with the national security that makes unnecessary a major arms buildup and the hostile political reaction it would engender among Japan's neighbors.

Regionalism is a force that is better defined in Europe than in Asia. This is mostly because of the presence of the European Community and the process of accelerating European integration in preparation for the elimination of all internal barriers in 1992. Furthermore, the EC has developed such a strong political momentum that formerly neutral states such as Sweden, Finland, and Austria, and possibly even Switzerland, have made formal applications for membership or are considering doing so. And as was true of Southern Europe in the late 1970s, the emerging democracies in Central Europe look to the EC rather than any individual European state as the political and economic anchor during their difficult period of transition. A united Germany will figure prominently in an integrating Europe. But Germany is unlikely to want to build a "Fortress Europe," a concept coined by Josef Goebbels and for that reason alone lacking political appeal and support in Germany.

Throughout the postwar era German foreign policy always sought to avoid having to choose between France and the United States, between the European and the Atlantic option. There is little indication that in the coming years German foreign policy will deviate from this past line. Both Germany's economic and security interests are best served by a closer European integration that does not isolate itself from the United States. In economic terms it would be outright foolish for one of the largest export nations in the world to favor building economic barriers. Furthermore, the success of American corporations operating in Europe in preparing for 1992 and the European investment strategy of Japanese firms in important industries such as automobiles show that trade protection is no longer a very effective instrument for isolating national or even regional markets.

Furthermore, the "EC 92" program excludes security policy. British and French interests may converge with German interests in building up one or several European options on questions of security policy. The political revival of the West European Union (WEU) and the growing importance of the European pillar in NATO reflect this fact. But German unification has probably increased French and British resolve to retain a national nuclear option and to keep the United States involved, both politically and militarily, in European affairs. Although France and Britain differ in their policy emphasis, on this basic point they agree and converge on German interests. NATO remains of fundamental importance in Germany's security policy. And so does an American presence in Europe, symbolically with ground forces and strategically with sea- and possibly air-based systems of nuclear deterrence, at least for the foreseeable future. For Germany, the CSCE is a potentially useful instrument of diplomacy that can supplement NATO and the EC because it avoids a narrow definition of Europe and keeps the United States as well as Canada and the Soviet Union involved in European and thus German security affairs.

Germany's weight in Europe and Europe's weight vis-à-vis the United States are, however, likely to increase both economically and politically. This redistribution in power is unlikely to find political articulation in military terms. Instead it will be fed by the compatibility between the German model of an efficient, capitalist, democratic welfare state and a political milieu of European states organized along similar lines and subscribing to similar political values. The compatibility between the German model and the

European milieu is substantial and ranks high as one of the most important German foreign policy objectives. This was very evident in the mid- and late 1970s when Germany took the most active role in trying to shape the process of transition to democracy in Southern Europe. The southern enlargement of the EC that contributed greatly to the success of that foreign policy provides something of a model with which Germany and its EC partners are approaching the daunting task of assisting the much more difficult process of transition in Central Europe. Similarly, in the 1980s the European Monetary System has been a very important instrument for establishing compatibility between Germany and Europe, largely on German terms. The stability of the deutsche mark and Germany's low inflation policy, at the cost of permanently high unemployment rates, became generalized throughout Europe. The conflicts over the technical aspects as well as the timing of the European Monetary Union are thus very important because they define the extent of compatibility between Germany and its European milieu.

In addition to European regionalism being better defined than Asian regionalism, it is politically more easily constructed. The EC has a well-institutionalized vision of European regionalism that is favored by the relative equality between Germany and the other major European powers. In Asia, however, institutions are relatively weak and of recent origin, and Japan towers over all of its neighbors with whom it might want to cooperate in a regional framework. It is significant that the United States will be part of both the emerging Asia and the new Europe, in economic terms no less than in security issues. As is true of Japan, the high-growth trajectory of many Asian states relies on the access to American markets. And the economic stake that American corporations have built up over decades in their European subsidiaries makes the United States a silent beneficiary of the EC 92 program. In the 1990s economic regions will be compatible with an integrating global economy. The U.S.-Japan security arrangement is an indispensable instrument for alleviating the quiet worries of Japan's Asian neighbors about Japan's rising power. And in Europe, through NATO, the United States will retain an important military and political voice that is welcomed by virtually all European states.

THE UNITED STATES
IN A WORLD OF REGIONS

How would the new regionalism that I have sketched in this chapter affect American foreign policy? Secretary of State Baker was very clear in his Berlin speech of December 12, 1989, that the United States no longer commands the resources to be the cornerstone of different world regions.[12] Here lies the great difference from the 1950s. But the United States also has no inclination to abdicate its interests and responsibilities in different regions and to move back to a position of isolation. That is the decisive difference from the 1930s. Instead, the United States has become an important pivot in a number of important regions. As part of Asia and Europe as well as of Latin America and the Middle East, it will act as an important regional power but will be unable to determine unilaterally the political shape of any one region, as is illustrated by the Mideast after the Gulf War.

This political role rests on America's military power, its economic presence, and its social appeal to important social strata overseas. The withdrawal of most American ground forces from Europe will return the United States in that part of the world to its natural role of a naval power. The outlines of a new NATO doctrine stressing mobile forces that can be deployed for purposes of intervention will rely on American intelligence, logistics, and transportation equipment but not on American ground troops. The decline of the North American economy has not impaired the competitiveness of America's global economy. American multinational corporations perform strongly in global markets and, together with Japanese corporations, are leading the world in the development of new technologies. Their strong presence in global markets gives American policymakers a strong incentive to maintain a liberal international economy. Finally, with English as the only universal language in the modern world, American mass culture has a natural advantage over all of its competitors in disseminating its products on a global scale and thus affecting the views of important social sectors in all societies.

America as a pivot is likely to be influenced in different ways by Europe and Asia. For example, in the case of Germany and Europe, problems of environmental security will rank high in coming years. The disastrous environmental problems in Central Europe are affecting an electorate in Western Europe that was already fully politicized around this issue in the 1980s. In the case of Japan and Asia, however, problems of technology, particularly militarily relevant high technologies, are likely to become a serious political issue. The United States will probably be affected more deeply by the Asian than the European challenge. Environmental problems and "new" security issues are viewed as less urgent in the United States than in Europe. Conversely, issues of technology transfer touching on "old" security issues are of decisive importance for the Department of Defense, one of the most important institutions in American politics. Different regions are likely to define different political problems that will affect the United States in different ways.

Furthermore, the United States is likely to use different political methods to deal with different regions. American-European relations are likely to rely often on multilateral diplomacy. NATO, the EC, and the CSCE among others all give some expression to a collective institutional and political identity of Europe, thus making multilateralism unavoidable. American-Asian relations are more likely to be a mixture of bilateral negotiations between the executive branch and different Asian governments on the one hand and unilateral actions of the U.S. Congress engaged in a perpetual power struggle with the executive and not bound by party loyalty on the other. European and Asian observers often credit American diplomacy with an evil genius for exploiting the difference between Congress and the president to maximum advantage in international negotiations. They overlook, however, the enormous liability of the policy immobilism that derives from this institutional and political fragmentation. As has been true in the past, a good foreign policy starts at home. The success of American foreign policy will depend critically on the success of adjusting to inescapable international problems through domestic policies.

The political pluralism of a world of regions means that the twenty-first century will be nobody's century. It will not be the century of America. It will not be the century of Europe. And it will not be the century of Asia. But in terms of interests, values, institutions, and political practices, each of these three regions will give the international system important political impulses. America will experiment with multiculturalism, Europe with the problems of environmentally sustainable forms of industrial life, and Asia with the development and marketing of new technologies.

But will these impulses be sufficiently strong? The new maps of the world that correct the distortions of the old Mercator map are showing the northern half of the world in a realistic, that is, much smaller, perspective. This corrective is essential if we want to understand the future shape of a world of regions. Because of his Eurocentric and Atlantic worldview, Hajo Holborn could not yet see the coming of a triregional world when he wrote in a brilliant book first published in 1951 that "the European political system has been replaced by the Atlantic political system."[13] Today it is already clear that the political regionalism of the North will have a chance to survive in the twenty-first century only if its political impulses are strong enough to envelop the South.

NOTES

1. Paul Kennedy, *The Rise and Fall of the Great Powers: Economic Change and Military Conflict from 1500 to 2000* (New York: Random House 1987).

2. Francis Fukuyama, "The End of History," in Kenneth M. Jensen, ed., *A Look at the End of History* (Washington, D.C.: U.S. Institute of Peace 1990), pp. 1–29.

3. Henry R. Nau, *The Myth of America's Decline: Leading the World Economy into the 1990s* (New York: Oxford University Press 1990); Joseph S. Nye, Jr., *Bound to Lead: The Changing Nature of American Power* (New York: Basic Books 1990).

4. John Mearsheimer, "Why We Will Soon Miss the Cold War," *The Atlantic* 266, no. 2 (August 1990), pp. 35–50; Kenneth N. Waltz, *Theory of International Politics* (Reading, Mass.: Addison-Wesley 1979).

5. U.S. Congress, Office of Technology Assessment, *Arming Our Allies: Cooperation and Competition in Defense Technology,* OTA-ISC-449 (Washington, D.C.: U.S. Government Printing Office 1990); U.S. Congress, Office of Technology Assessment, *Global Arms Trade: Commerce in Advanced Military Technology and Weapons,* OTA-ISC-460 (Washington, D.C.: U.S. Government Printing Office 1991).

6. Shintaro Ishihara, *The Japan That Can Say No: Why Japan Will Be First Among Equals* (New York: Simon and Schuster 1991).

7. George Friedman and Meredith LeBard, *The Coming War with Japan* (New York: St. Martin's 1991).

8. Mearsheimer, "Why We Will Soon Miss the Cold War," pp. 35–50.

9. Esyn Hamaguchi, "A Contextual Model of the Japanese: Toward a Methodological Innovation in Japan Studies," *Journal of Japanese Studies* 11 (1985), pp. 289–321.

10. George Orwell, *Nineteen Eighty-Four: A Novel* (New York: Harcourt, Brace and World 1949).

11. Bruce Cumings, "The Origins and Development of the Northeast Asian Political Economy: Industrial Sectors, Product Cycles, and Political Consequences," in Frederic C. Deyo, ed., *The Political Economy of the New Asian Industrialism* (Ithaca: Cornell University Press 1987), pp. 44–83.

12. Secretary of State James A. Baker, address to Berlin Press Club, "A New Europe, a New Atlanticism: Architecture for a New Era," December 12, 1989, Department of State, *Current Policy,* no. 1233 (1989).

13. Hajo Holborn, *The Collapse of Europe* (New York: Knopf 1960), p. 192.

8

Trading States in a New Concert of Europe

Richard N. Rosecrance

Will there be a new Concert of Europe[1] in the future? To answer this question, one must recall the precedents of at least two previous attempts at such diplomatic groupings: the first after the Congress of Vienna and the second after World War I. Both efforts ultimately failed. If a new Concert can succeed today, it will bring great diplomatic and economic benefit to both domestic and international affairs in the years ahead. If such a Concert is to thrive, it will depend upon the farsighted policy of the European Community, its member states, and associated countries. This Concert of Nations, though centered upon Europe as a crucial supporting pillar, will become worldwide in scope and embrace the United States, Japan, the Soviet Union (or a new Russian Federation), and other nations as well. An integrating Europe will remain as the cornerstone of this cooperation. In an extension of the architectural metaphor, Europe will become the keystone of the arch uniting East and West in world politics.

EUROPE AND THE TRADING MODEL

Why will Europe be so important? There are essentially two reasons: First, Europe is proving in the relationships of the member countries of the European Community (and also in its relations with the associated European Free Trade Area in the European Economic Area) that it can be a practical model of how countries are brought into regular economic and political cooperation with one another. Second, European states are "trading states" that seek their livelihoods through international commerce rather than through military or territorial expansion. They thereby constitute an exemplar of the manner in which peaceful countries can interact.

Here the model of the enlargement of the Community is even more important than its deepening in integrative terms. In order to join Europe, countries must be democratic and politically stable, must possess flexible and to a large degree free market economies with considerable transparency, and must be capable of renouncing past enmities and animosities. In the terms of the American international relations theorist Karl Deutsch, such an association must be in effect a "pluralistic security community" where war among members has been for all practical purposes ruled out.[2] Sectarian or ethnic nationalism and irredentism is inconsistent with membership in a European federation.[3]

Europe's model of association among nations breaks new ground even if the eventual relationship of member nations achieves less than full integration and the abolition of the national state as a sovereign entity.[4] Europe has pioneered in creating and sustaining democratic "trading states" that no longer harbor aggressive territorial designs at the expense of one another but that, in contrast, seek their livelihood through economic development sustained by foreign trade.[5] As a congeries of trading units, Europe has more completely fulfilled the model of a trading state than has Japan, which still retains important mercantilist elements in its trading practices.[6] With the exception of a still highly protected agricultural sector, European trading states have readjusted their own domestic structures to conform with international market pressures.[7] Japan, however, still seeks to force a large part of the adjustment process onto foreign competitors.[8]

It remains true of both Europe and Japan (to say nothing of the rising countries of the Pacific Rim) that "trading states" (*Handelsstaaten*) have different political and military interests from past territorial states.[9] Nations that decide to pursue their livelihoods through trade rather than through military expansion can concentrate their energies on investment in new products and prosper in the world marketplace as a consequence.[10] Nations that continue to place major stress upon military defense (or resistance to military threats) or that seek continued options for territorial expansion generally distort and limit their own economic growth.[11] But the positive side of the trading vocation is that it can broaden and strengthen the political relationships among participating countries.

How might this take place? First, trading states depend upon a relatively open international trading system. High tariffs, exchange controls, quotas, and "beggar-thy-neighbor" policies are inconsistent with such a system. Financial openness is equally important. Countries in an open trading system must have the option of securely investing in each other, for both short- and long-term purposes. Through the free movement of capital, they are allowed to prosper from foreign investments as they would from investments at home. The right to repatriate profits and to bring back invested capital is inherent in such a system.

Second, trading states achieve their defense not by autarky but by association with other like-minded nations, thereby conserving national expenditure. With the possible exception of the United States, which spent a relatively high fraction of its gross national product on defense during its past forty years' participation in the North Atlantic Alliance,[12] allied states could economize on military appropriations because each nation did not have to face a whole range of military contingencies by itself. One nation could rely on its partners to assist in air or naval strength, nuclear or conventional weapons, thereby lessening its own military budget.

Third, mature trading states recognize that there will never be a time when they will become powerful or self-sufficient enough to risk casting off their economic and military ties with other nations. In this sense full independence and freedom of action is not a realistic possibility for trading states in international politics. In the late nineteenth century, this did not appear to be true. Then, some new industrial states, using a strategy of export-led growth to fashion a surplus in world markets, sought eventually to break the ties of interdependence that bound them to the international economy. The benefits of late industrial development, which Germany and Japan experienced in the nineteenth century, caused them to think that territorial gains could reduce their dependence on external markets and resources.

Today, however, late twentieth century trading nations are not capable of resuming full self-sufficiency at a later stage. The example of the Soviet Union underscores the point. Russia, a late developer, gained many advantages in industrial progress in the 1890s and in the first decade of the twentieth century. It was the largest state in territorial terms—a veritable continent in size, stretching over eleven time zones. Its resources of oil and minerals seemed endless, and under the tsars it was one of the world's leading agricultural exporters. Anticipating Alexander Gerschenkron's theory that late developers have key advantages,[13] in the five-year plans starting in 1928 Stalin sought to capture the most advanced Western designs and apparently believed that he could proceed from there without further reliance on the outside world. It was not until 1985 that Gorbachev realized that this was impossible. When this was understood, Russia sought to be readmitted to the international trading system and the fraternity of nations. It appears that an economy developing in isolation from the world trading system will eventually fall behind. The German failure to recognize this reality under the ministrations of Hjalmar Schacht slowed Nazi economic and technological development.

Even an integrated Europe after 1994 and later will not be large enough to be self-sufficient in trade, technology, and resources. It will still depend upon a wider world economy. It will still rely upon investments within other tariff zones to provide access to markets and technology that are not available in Europe. It will require exports to countries outside of Europe to pay for needed energy imports. American and Japanese customers will continue to be very important for an integrated Europe. A united Europe will still have to import large amounts of oil from the Persian Gulf.

What unique role does an integrating Europe have to play in these developments? As I have said, Europe is the cornerstone of the system in the sense that it is the economic lodestone that attracts nearby countries to cooperate and associate with it. It was not just the attractions of the Western international economy that beckoned to Gorbachev, but the practical advantages of developing a closer economic and political relationship with Europe—obtaining European aid, penetrating European markets, taking advantage of European technology and marketing skills, learning financial savoir faire from sophisticated European money centers.

The Soviet Union could build a supersonic transport. But it could not commercialize this technology so that it could be sold to other countries. (It is interesting, however, to note that the Soviet aircraft manufacturer Sukhoi has now undertaken to build and market a supersonic executive jet in association with Gulfstream Aerospace, an American company.) New links with Western companies do not change the general rule that Soviet and Russian leaders need to learn a great deal more before they will be able to commercialize technology (or to even learn what technology to develop) and to create new products to sell to the West and to a wider world.[14]

Today strategic trade theory teaches that a country does not have to depend upon comparative advantage, as it did in the past, to find its niche in international trade. Rather, it can make novel investments that create long-term returns from expanding markets in other countries. With an energetic and well-trained labor force, a nation can essentially create its own advantage. Countries can focus on high-technology investments that will preempt a market that others are about to enter. Japan had no comparative advantage in building or creating the 16k chip, but once it did so it could get markets for the 64k and 256k chip: It created new markets in advanced memory chips that soon gave it world leadership. If Japan had not built the 16k chip, it would not have been able to compete with the United States on a long-term basis and would have lost out at the beginning of the development of the new technology.[15] It tends to follow that countries that strive to isolate themselves from the world market and associated trends in technology may end up falling behind.

THE REVERSAL OF
THE BALANCE OF POWER

The Soviet Union wanted to associate itself with Europe and also the wider capitalist world to keep up with these new economic and technological developments. As far as Europe is concerned, this association is significant because in microcosm it mirrors the new centripetal tendencies of the international system as a whole. Outsiders or nations on the fringe of Europe seek to participate in technological and market developments occurring inside Europe. As a result, Europe as an integrative magnet is reversing the centuries-old tradition of the balance of power. It is drawing countries in toward a growing core of power in world politics.[16]

In traditional *Realpolitik*, the increase of European power might have been expected to force the Soviet Union or Eastern Europe to balance against that power, even more than a traditional alliance would have done. European integration actually creates greater concentration of strength because, as opposed to alliance, it welds separate national units together in economic and industrial terms. It is surprising that no balancing takes place against it. Because that power is not military or hegemonic in nature but is rather the economic power of an association of trading states that are legally and to some degree constitutionally linked, an integrated Europe does not drive other states away (through balancing mechanisms) but instead attracts them. Europe does not seek to expand its borders territorially, and, indeed, it very reluctantly responds to petitions of others that wish to join the European center of power. Its power attracts; it does not repel.

Europe has pioneered in creating the only fully successful instance of a customs union among modern industrial countries.[17] If countries that join such a union pursue similar fiscal and monetary policies, the trade balance among them tends to become skewed in one direction. If they are not open to each others' inspection, reliable statistics on the interchange between them cannot be gathered. These statistics form the basis for the agreement on regulations to govern trade and social policy. Procedures for assessing tax or enhanced value at the frontier for goods that were partly manufactured abroad must be agreed upon. In short, a customs union requires a great deal of trust and openness among participating nations. It is not surprising that customs unions (e.g., the *Zollverein* in the 1830s) have been precursors to full political integration. Even economic associations, like those in the European Free Trade Area (EFTA), for instance, required a much greater discipline in national economic policy and a greater give-and-take among countries than normally takes place among sovereign states. Thus the very process of integration itself, even if it should fall short of political union, brings countries closer together.

The policy of customs unions is generally inward-looking and peaceful in character. Countries bent on solving the problems that are associated with establishing links of free trade areas among themselves are generally not in a position to think of external aggression.[18] As customs unions move to further economic integration they develop new federal economic institutions in which countries have to consent to major changes in national policy. The institutional setting itself means that sudden military measures by one member have to be accepted de facto by the other participants, as the nations of the European Community agreed to British action in the Falklands in 1982. Such institutions do not lend themselves to the creation of an expanded military hegemony over other nearby nations. Thus the European Community has developed relations with candidate member states that are both open and peaceful in character. Neighbors do not fear "Euro-imperialism." When Poland was worried about Germany's ambitions to reacquire its Eastern territories, it was at least partly reassured by the continued embedding of a united Germany in the integrated Europe. A further deepening of the integration would add further reassurance.

THE CONCERT OF POWERS

In the past, the basis for a successful Concert of Europe resided in a core of powerful and united nations that sought to remain in association with one another to consult and decide on international developments. This core never continued for more than a decade or so; the center never held together. Despite a series of successful European Congresses after 1815, the Concert weakened after 1822 when the United Kingdom ceased to associate closely with Russia and Austria. England returned to an isolationist policy under George Canning. It refused, in particular, to intervene within the domestic affairs of European states, despite the persuasions of Klemens Count Metternich.

In the second abortive episode, the United States returned to a policy of isolation in 1920, and Britain and France were left alone to face an aggrieved Germany and unappeased German nationalism. The American refusal to ratify the Versailles Treaty nullified the effectiveness of the League Council; it also canceled the Treaty of Guarantee with France and Britain, and the United States no longer participated in the political and military balance in Europe.

But the withdrawal or isolation of key countries was not the only reason for the ineffectiveness of previous Concerts of powers. In both cases the world economy did not develop in such a way as to unite the two halves of Europe and sustain political cooperation. In the first half of the nineteenth century, Great Britain was in the throes of the Industrial Revolution. It exported to the continent, but following a high tariff policy until the late 1840s, Britain initially did not take a large share of continental products in trade. Britain directed many of its new manufactured goods to Europe but tended to buy from the New World and the Empire. In the latter part of the nineteenth century, the situation reversed. Britain turned ever more to Empire and to the outside world to sell its goods, turning its back on Europe.

As a result, Britain lessened its economic stake in the relationship with Europe. Compared to its investments in the empire and in the developing world, the United Kingdom had a small liquid stake invested in European economies. It could and did sell its shares quickly with the onset of war in 1914.

In the second episode mentioned, the United States turned its back on the continent until the Dawes and Young plans, but when these failed, it did not cooperate with others to revive the economy of still-liberal Weimar Germany.[19] The Fordney-McCumber (1922) and Smoot-Hawley (1930) tariffs made it difficult, indeed impossible, for European countries to sell enough in the United States to repay war debts and German loans. The Europeans were ultimately forced to default on debts and reparations payments to the United States at the Lausanne Conference in 1932. America then compounded the error in 1933 by devaluing the dollar.

For both political and economic reasons, in neither of these cases did the core hold together. A Concert of Europe and a League of Nations Council could not continue to function in any effective way.

There are three reasons why failure of the present Concert experiment is somewhat less likely to occur in the future. First, no key actor has left the core of the international system in the aftermath of the 1989 success and the end of the Cold War. Arguments to the contrary notwithstanding, the United States will not leave Europe in the lurch,[20] and the German military training bases in the United States signal the reciprocity and equality of the defense arrangements between the two countries. Through NATO, the CSCE, and other arrangements, the United States will remain a participant in the military and security affairs of Europe.[21] The Gulf War perhaps demonstrates how the American people can respond to security threats in other, and ostensibly less important, areas of the world than Europe.

There are, however, those who do not accept this analysis and contend that the United States will neither continue to associate itself with an integrated Europe, nor will it be needed. France has sometimes argued that a Europe of the twelve is completely self-sufficient in security, based as that security would be on French and British nuclear weapons. This contention is understandable, given the weakness of the present-day Soviet Union and the disarray in Eastern Europe. One must recall, however, that the Concerts of the past, as well as directing affairs in Europe, sustained an equilibrium within their number. Although the Concert lent a quasi-governing authority to international relations and to smaller powers, its successful functioning depended upon a tolerable balance inside the Concert mechanism. In 1815, Russia and Prussia proposed to carve up a new and tempting territorial dish at the Congress of Vienna. Prussia would gain Saxony and Russia would take Poland. When Austria, Britain, and even France heard of the proposed "Polish-Saxon deal," they immediately agreed to resist any such one-sided outcome. When confronted with this opposition, Russia and Prussia gave up the project. Thus the existence of a balance within the Concert served to keep it functioning effectively and harmoniously.

In the future the twelve European nations may not be quite as self-sufficient in security as present events suggest. As East European countries strive to associate themselves with the institutions in Brussels, the Soviet Union (or its successor state) will also be drawn in as a participant. Two issues are important here; one is short term in character and the other is long term. Although events appear to be moving toward a peaceful resolution of the difficulties between Moscow-center and the nine cooperating republics, a breakdown cannot be entirely ruled out. The Russian military abetted by the old party cadres might reassert or try to reassert itself to prevent a further devolution of power to the provinces. The process might not be an entirely peaceful one, and one cannot entirely dismiss the possibility of a reemergence of a party-army regime in the Soviet Union. In such a case, the reassuring presence of American forces might provide both a political and military deterrence that would be needed to guarantee that the new regime does not seek to move to reassert its control of Eastern Europe. Even without such apocalyptic events taking place, in time a resurgent Russia will emerge, in both economic and political terms. Such renewed strength could translate itself into a stronger military position as well. If this occurred, there would no longer be a balance within the Concert, and the Europe of the twelve would need the active assistance of the United States to help maintain its internal equilibrium.

In addition, a Europe confined to the twelve (with other associate members) would be too weak to play a central role in world politics generally. It could not strictly constitute a core to which other nations would be drawn. It might, unfortunately, only concentrate so much power as to stimulate a balancing response against it by excluded states. Here the reaction of Japan and China could be critical in determining the outcome. Only with American participation does a European core of power emerge; only thus does balance give way to attraction so far as the rest of the system is concerned. For systemic as well as European reasons, the United States needs to remain associated with Europe in a strong central coalition.

But not all the reasons for the continuance and strength of the Concert are negative (that key players will not withdraw or be asked to leave). The second, more important, reason for the solidity of the core is that countries have a far greater economic stake in the prosperity of one another than was true in 1815, 1920, or 1945. And it even appears that economic deterrence is beginning to substitute for military deterrence as a stabilizing force in international politics.

It is perhaps worth recalling that military and nuclear deterrence is a very crude influence strategy. With the development of intercontinental nuclear missiles, the Soviet Union holds the American population at risk and the United States holds the Soviet population hostage. Because these "hostages" are not within the territorial jurisdiction of the enemy power, they cannot be influenced by carrot or stick or persuaded to change their attitude. The choice is that of an "on-off" switch: "to kill or not to kill" the population of the adversary. Russian influence upon U.S. policy is thus entirely negative in character; it is also very gross.

Economic deterrence refers to the stake that one country holds within another in terms of markets and productive investments. If that stake is a broadly symmetrical one, then each country has much to lose if the other's economy does not prosper. The influence process is a much more subtle one: The home economy can influence and reshape the foreign economy's stake through tax and expenditure policy—inhibitive or enabling legislation. Unlike the situation in military deterrence in which the "hostage" resides outside the political and legal borders of the home country, in economic deterrence the stake or hostage exists within the host's domestic jurisdiction. In addition, a government can decide to reward foreign investment and exports as well as to punish them. The influence is both positive and negative. As the stake that individual trading units hold within the confines of another's economy rise in value and symmetry, deterrent mechanisms progressively come to interdict the outbreak of radical economic conflict. The importance of these mechanisms should not be understated.

In a pair of studies a few years ago, Cornell University investigators examined the pattern of cooperation among the Group of Six (the United States, Japan, the German Federal Republic, France, Britain, and Canada) in international monetary negotiations from 1960 to 1970.[22] In each case a measure was prepared of the amount of cooperation each nation gave and received in the negotiations. This was then correlated with a series of indicators of economic influence or power, such as growth rates, size of foreign exchange holdings, trade balance, and the like. The formal results were negative. What turned out to be much more influential than these indicators of economic power was the degree to which one country had a foreign investment stake in the economic success of another country. At that time the United States had a significant Foreign Direct Investment (FDI) stake in the fate of European economies. Although this stake was not yet fully reciprocal, European direct investment in the United States remained quite low. It was not surprising that European countries—France and Germany—did particularly well, receiving a great deal of cooperation in the negotiations. The United States was in the middle. Last of all, of course, was Japan, the country in whose economy no other country had been allowed to develop a significant stake, either in export markets or direct investment in Japanese productive assets. Fortunately, today Japan has become aware of the problem and is seeking to draw in imports through a domestic stimulus strategy and also to permit greater foreign and direct investment in the Japanese economy. It appears, therefore, that with the possible exception of China and Russia, each major industrial economy is today extending its stake in the economies of other nations. Production is being internationalized and a greater proportion of erstwhile national production is now taking place outside of national borders. According to Japanese estimates, American production overseas may now be nearing 20 percent of U.S. domestic production. Japanese production abroad has increased from 2 percent of gross national product to something like 7 percent. These figures will increase further as Europe integrates and the North American Free Trade Area develops and expands.

The net effect of growing and reciprocal economic stakes among major world trading units is to deter the outbreak of economic conflict between them. A fully symmetrical pattern would guarantee to impoverish any economic aggressor, preventing a repetition of the economic conflict of the 1930s in the later 1990s.

Some observers, of course, will disagree with this conclusion, citing the interdependencies of European economies in 1913. Foreign trade was then already a very high proportion of gross national product for Britain, France, and Germany. Despite high continental tariffs, markets were relatively open. Capital moved easily between financial centers, though of course it never equalized interest rates among leading nations. But the stake of individual economies in the fates of others was distinctly limited. Investment was by and large portfolio in character; it was not direct investment, which involves a significant percentage ownership of the foreign firm. Portfolio instruments could easily be disposed of on the stock exchanges of Europe. The much more illiquid direct investment (investment in the ownership and management of productive facilities in another country) was not common. Thus, in fact, the degree of financial interdependence among the three central countries in 1913 has been greatly overstated. Although Britain, France, and Germany traded extensively with one another, each nation hoped to use its imperial ties increasingly to substitute for reliance upon a European market. In an era of "imperial federationalist" tendencies, Britain and other countries thought of the Empire as an independent unit. Among such empires, trading relations were much less important and the economic interdependencies also were reduced.

It has also been noted that in 1939 Britain and Germany engaged in substantial international trade with one another. This high level of trade did not prevent war in 1939. But trade as a proportion of the gross national product had fallen precipitately in the interim because of the depression and the consequent imposition of restrictions upon trade. Well into its rearmament plan, Germany depended much less upon trade with the outside world than it had in 1928. Japan was seeking self-sufficiency in its Co-Prosperity Sphere in China and East Asia. Nations were not restrained from military expansion because of trading ties. Rather, they hoped to acquire through the use of military force the resources they had previously been dependent upon trade to obtain. Because self-sufficiency was not totally beyond the bounds of possibility at the low levels of economic production existing at the depths of the depression, the remaining, rather restricted, amount of economic interdependence was a force for war, not peace, among nations.

Third, a new European Concert is likely to continue to function because it will draw in other countries, if not to fully integrative arrangements at least to the association of a customs union (though not, I believe a currency union).[23] After EFTA (Austria, Norway, Finland, Sweden, Switzerland, and Iceland) is granted membership, Poland, Hungary, and Czechoslovakia will join. The three East European countries will have to participate because they will need to reorient their trade to the West instead of the Soviet Union and they will need special trade concessions to develop and stabilize their economies. Hence they will depend upon access to the Community market. Well after them will come the Russian federation and the Baltics (which also need access to European markets). The Soviet successor state or federation will probably not be able (at least initially) to compete on the basis of free and equal access to world markets. It will require European capital and a place to sell its goods on relatively favorable terms. It must then develop new products that can be sold on a worldwide basis. The raw material basis of its economy will be transformed. Given political and economic liberalization, I can foresee it eventually developing an associate status in the common European market.

The larger Europe that would develop in this context would be more likely to form a customs than a currency union. The participation of East European nations, perhaps Morocco and Turkey, and the association with the Soviet Union would inevitably mean that Europe's integrative character would be somewhat less pronounced than what might have been attained in a smaller, more homogeneous federation. It would then be difficult to conceive that full political union could be achieved among such a diverse group of states. Thus although the nations of Europe would have strongly confederal economic ties, they might not have a single political decisionmaking center. The member nations would not then have completely given up their separate diplomatic or military powers.[24]

If this is true, even the European pillar of the world Concert of powers will represent a genuine Concert of nations, with members playing their separate parts but retaining a degree of autonomy and independence. Especially in foreign policy matters or in defense questions occurring outside the community, it is difficult to imagine the member nations resigning their individual functions to an all-powerful decisionmaking center in Brussels. This does not mean, however, that members will not have to consult one another to implement plans that would involve a large diversion of resources from Europe to other areas.

IMPLICATIONS FOR A WIDER WORLD

If Europe continues to enlarge and the economic space grows proportionately, and if the United States continues to remain involved in European economic and military affairs, the world may be on the threshold of a new, more peaceful era. If this development proceeds, it will mean not merely that the core of nations will not break up but also that it will be further strengthened. Then, as a result of mutual links with the European Community, the central coalition in world politics will consist of Europe, the United States, and the Soviet Union.

This coalition will be too strong, economically and militarily, for other nations to stand against it. Thus Japan and China will not be tempted to form a grouping to balance against it; instead they will be tempted to try to join it. Because Japan and China are both exporting powers, their domestic economies will not, at least for the foreseeable future, be able to absorb the total production of Japanese and Chinese factories and mines. China may pose a particularly difficult problem here. It appears that Beijing will be even more reluctant to open up its domestic economy to outside investment and foreign imports than Japan has been. Political liberalization in China will certainly lag behind that of other trading nations, perhaps even behind that of a politically modernizing Russian federation. It is therefore imperative that the economies of Europe and North America follow a common approach toward their Asian competitors. Ultimately it is the market potential of North America and an enlarging Europe that will play the greatest role in bringing economic (and possibly political) change to Beijing. China will not willingly end its mercantilist policies. It must be persuaded and induced to do so. Here the well-developed European approach—governing trade with outside powers—will be even more sensitive to Chinese mercantilism than America has yet been. Its standards will influence those finally adopted by the United States.

In the same way, the Brussels response to the Japanese trade challenge and local content requirements will probably also affect

U.S. standards. In time, both North America and Europe will come to favor local production over foreign exports, and neither will tolerate the existence of foreign assembly plants in their market. High-technology work will have to be performed within the tariff zone and technology itself transferred to Europe and North America in the form of patents. These joint pressures will have a continuing intrusive effect in Japan and China, persuading Tokyo and Beijing to dismantle many of their existing restrictions and policies. Then the economic stake of European and American companies in the Japanese and Chinese market can increase through the purchase of Japanese and Chinese companies. Direct investment will jump over the tariff barrier and make possible much greater European and American participation in the economic prosperity of Japan and China. The symmetry of economic stakes will greatly increase.

As Japan and China are progressively drawn into the original core, consisting of Europe, the United States, and Russia, the strength of a world Concert of powers will grow. The attractions of this now larger and more cohesive grouping will also have an influence upon the Third World. This powerful political and economic magnet will attract Third World nations as well.

As we know, in the heydays of *dependencia* thinking, the nations of the Third World wanted to opt out and decouple their links with the Northern world economy. Now, as Mexico has found out, it is better to join it than to try to survive in economic isolation. Brazil and Argentina are reentering it, though Brazil still has formidable problems with opening up its government-controlled economy. In time, India will be forced to do so as well—the advantages of trade with the Western economy are demonstrated by the examples of Thailand and Malaysia.

However, this may not be the final word on the degree of political and economic conflict in world politics generally and in regard to the integrating Europe. Some observers are quite worried that the formation of three new trading blocs could actually set the stage for a new round of international economic strife.[25] They believe that this could lead to the collapse of the core and the end of the world Concert of nations.

But this pessimistic result is unlikely for reasons that I have partly sketched above. Consider just for a moment what impact the creation of new trading blocs has upon international economic politics. It may cut down on exports from one bloc to another, but it will greatly increase foreign direct investment in each of the blocs. Countries that cannot be sure of exporting to the bloc (over the tariff barrier) will compensate for that as they did after 1957 by investing directly within the bloc and producing there. As a result, their stake in the economies of the bloc may be no less than before. FDI would merely have substituted for exports. Export markets would still remain very important. In the short term, domestic corporations cannot be adequately compensated, but multinational firms can. It is possible over time to endeavor to reorient export markets, as Japan is now trying to do, partially substituting Asian for North American customers. Yet a country's economic stake in a particular market may be greater via the mechanism of foreign direct investment than it is via exports. It is harder to shift productive facilities than marketing arrangements for goods produced elsewhere. When the United States went into producing in the European market after 1957, it made a relatively permanent commitment to that market. In this sense, the investment in the new trading bloc will enhance the outside investing countries' dependence on the economic performance of the bloc economy itself. We should therefore expect trading blocs to create rather than to substitute for existing interdependencies.

Such blocs will not be autonomous or economically self-sufficient. These claims are buttressed by statistical comparisons (see Table 8.1).

Although Europe has become more self-sufficient in trade (though not in investment), its dependence upon energy imports continues at a high level, as shown by Table 8.2. It is difficult if not impossible to think that Europe could ever become self-sufficient in energy.

Economic stakes of one nation or trading unit in another are strengthened by the pattern of investment. Unfortunately, the statistics for this are typically incommensurable, but we do know that the U.S. investment stake in Europe is very large and that of Europe and Japan in the United States is growing rapidly. The most pronounced asymmetry occurs in American and European direct investment in Japan, which, because of Japanese restrictions, remains much lower than Japanese investment in America and Europe. Table 8.3 gives general (though not always particular) figures.

These figures help to establish a few central points. Japan is extremely dependent upon foreign trade and is growing dependent upon its foreign investment abroad as well. It must sell 36 percent of its exports every year in the U.S. market. No other country takes more than 6 percent of Japanese exports. It will therefore be very difficult for Japan to sell its North American–bound products somewhere else. The Japanese economy may actually be twice as large as it needs to be solely to serve the needs of the Japanese domestic population. It is difficult to believe that an East Asian trading bloc

TABLE 8.1   Percentage of Export Dependence on Particular Markets, 1986 and 1989

	1986	1989
European Community on U.S. market	9.29	7.45
United States on EC market	24.46	23.80
Japan on U.S. market	38.88	34.22
Japan on EC market[a]	17.00	

[a]Approximation for 1986; no 1989 figure available.

SOURCES: IMF, *Direction of Trade Statistics, Yearbook 1986* (Washington, D.C.: IMF, 1986); IMF, *International Financial Statistics Yearbook 1990* (Washington, D.C.: IMF, 1990).

TABLE 8.2   Annual Energy Imports as a Percentage of Total Consumption, 1985 and 1988

	1985	1988
EEC total	43.85	47.51
Germany	50.64	53.19

SOURCE: *Energy, Statistical Yearbook 1987*, 1988.

TABLE 8.3   Worldwide Foreign Direct Investments by Source and Target, 1988 (percentage of total)

	As Source of Investment	As Target of Investment
United States	31.7	33.4
Japan	10.7	NA
United Kingdom	17.8	9.7
West Germany	9.4	NA
Developing countries	NA	25.9
Asia (including Japan)	NA	7.3

Note: Total world direct investment for 1988 was $1.03 trillion.

SOURCE: *1990 Jetro White Paper on Foreign Direct Investment,* March 1990, p. 2.

could provide Japan with the market that it presently enjoys in the United States and Europe.

The United States is also heavily dependent upon foreign markets (though not yet as dependent as Japan). It must sell 23 percent of its exports each year within the European Community. It is difficult to imagine conditions under which all U.S. exports to Europe could suddenly be sold in Latin America or Canada. Most self-sufficient is the European market area. Member countries export mainly to themselves. But Europe is not fully independent. It must import about 50 percent of its energy needs. It is not self-sufficient in technology, certainly not in computers, electronics, software, or biotechnology. It is dependent upon returns from the huge foreign direct investment, which it maintains within the market of other blocs, principally North America.

Thus the creation of new trading blocs will not provide economic self-sufficiency. The central sponsors of these blocs—Japan, Germany, and the United States—remain heavily dependent upon nations and markets outside of their customs zones. Their stake in each other remains very high, and further direct investment will maintain that stake even if trade seems to diminish it. In other words, the conditions for a continuing Concert of major powers, centered on Europe, will likely endure. Historically, no such association existed among the members of previous European and international Concerts. Members all too often thought of going it alone, economically speaking, or, if that was impossible, of creating an empire or imperial arrangements that would make the unit as a whole practically self-sufficient. Present-day trading blocs do not have that objective and they will not gain self-sufficiency in any event.

As a result, the history of the balance of power will have to be rewritten in the twenty-first century to admit the possibility and actuality of major nations joining together in an enhanced and enlarged Concert of Europe that actually endures. The establishment of a core of nations in a central coalition will actually serve to draw others in, not to repulse them. This does not mean that such a grouping will endure forever, but it may last long enough to allow nations to think about an even more enduring constitutional association in the years ahead.

NOTES

1. A Concert of Europe is an association of nations in which the national members still retain independent diplomatic decisionmaking powers (even though the Concert itself is endowed with such powers for particular purposes). A Concert does not become a "core" of a "central coalition" until it arrogates more than half of the power in the entire world system of states.

2. Karl W. Deutsch, Sidney A. Burrell, Robert A. Kann, Maurice Lee, Jr., Martin Lichtermann, Raymond E. Lindren, Francis L. Loewenheim, Richard W. Van Wagenen, *Political Community and the North Atlantic Area* (Princeton: Princeton University Press 1957); Emmanuel Adler, *Europe's Pacific Union: A Pluralistic Security Community* (Berkeley: University of California Press 1991).

3. Jack Snyder, "Hypernationalism," unpublished manuscript, 1991.

4. National policymakers have three tools to shape economic outcomes: the control of capital flows, the setting of exchange rates, and the control of monetary policy. The Mundell-Fleming conditions suggest that they can utilize only two of the three. If after the period from 1992 to 1994 European national decisionmakers agree to accept freedom of capital movements and

concede their control over exchange rates (in the ERM [exchange rate mechanism] and EMS [European Monetary System]), they can no longer set independent monetary policy for their country. A number of states, not only Britain, will be reluctant to lose such powers and European integration thus may be circumscribed.

5. Richard Rosecrance, *America's Economic Resurgence: A Bold New Strategy* (New York: HarperCollins 1990).

6. Karel Van Wolferen, *The Enigma of Japanese Power* (London: Macmillan 1989).

7. Peter Katzenstein, *Small States and World Markets* (Ithaca: Cornell University Press 1985); Ronald Rogowsky, *Commerce and Coalitions* (Princeton: Princeton University Press 1990).

8. Clyde Prestowitz, *Trading Places* (New York: Basic Books 1988).

9. Richard Rosecrance, *The Rise of the Trading State: Commerce and Conquest in the Modern World* (New York: Basic Books 1986); see Rosecrance, *America's Economic Resurgence*.

10. Leslie Gelb, "Memo for Mr. Bush," *New York Times,* June 12, 1991, p. A19.

11. Paul Kennedy, *The Rise and Fall of the Great Powers* (New York: Random House 1987); Robert DeGrasse, Jr., *Military Expansion, Economic Decline* (New York: M. E. Sharpe 1983); Jack Hirshleifer, "The Paradox of Power," UCCLA Department of Economics, manuscript, June 1991. Hirshleifer points out that where decisive military results will not occur, weak countries may benefit from challenging stronger ones militarily. At a low level of economic product, they may gain more militarily than they lose economically.

12. Mancur Olson and Richard Zeckhauser, "An Economic Theory of Alliances," *Review of Economics and Statistics* 48, no. 3, (1966), pp. 266–279.

13. Alexander Gerschenkron, *Economic Backwardness in Historical Perspective: A Book of Essays* (Cambridge: Belknap Press of Harvard University Press 1962).

14. Paul Krugman, *Rethinking International Trade* (Cambridge: M.I.T. Press 1990).

15. It does not follow from this that a lead in one type of technology necessarily produces an advantage in other types. The typical DRAM or microprocessor did not absolutely grant gains in RISC chips. Nations could always leap in when new technologies were started.

16. "Balance of power" refers to relationships among nations where no core of power at the center of the system has yet been created. A core of power exists when so much centralized power already exists in one grouping that balancing will not be effective against it (that is, the sum of the remaining power in the system is less than that arrogated in the core). Power repels in balance situations; power attracts in core situations.

17. Experience with the North American Free Trade Area is still too sketchy to render a definitive judgment in that case.

18. Napoleon's "Continental System" of 1807, however, may represent an exception. Of course, in the Napoleonic case France already dominated Europe and did not have to negotiate with equals to establish its economic policies

and programs. Institutionally it did not need their consent to new military actions. The establishment of a customs union with Canada also did not restrain U.S. action in the Gulf War.

19. Stephen Schuker, "American Reparations to Germany, 1919–1933" (Princeton: International Finance Section, Department of Economics, Princeton University Press 1988).

20. John Mearsheimer, "Will We Soon Miss the Cold War?" *The Atlantic* 266, no. 2 (August 1990).

21. Secretary of State James A. Baker, "The Euro-Atlantic Architecture; From West to East," address to the Aspen Institute Berlin, June 18, 1991, Department of State, press release, June 18, 1991.

22. William Gutowitz, "The Interrelationship of Economic Factors and Political Relations Among Nations: A Quantitative Analysis," honor's thesis, Cornell University 1978; Brian Healy, "Economic Transition in the International System: The Translation of Economic Power into Political Leverage in the International Monetary System," Ph.D. dissertation, Cornell University, 1973.

23. See Note 4.

24. The United Kingdom has already formally rejected a part of the draft treaty for a political union in Europe. See *Financial Times,* June 18, 1991, p. 1.

25. Robert Gilpin, *The Political Economy of International Relations* (Princeton: Princeton University Press 1987).

9

America's European Agenda: Learning from the Past and Creating for the Future

Catherine McArdle Kelleher

The revolutions of 1989 present the United States with a unique historical opportunity: the chance to revisit the definition of national interest and national security that it made in the fateful years of 1945 to 1949. Nowhere is the opportunity more dramatic than in Europe, the price and the prize throughout four decades of Cold War competition. Gone are the organizing principles of anticommunism and containment. What is needed now is a new definition of basic American interests in Europe that allows the United States to overcome its past habits of political dominance and reliance on the NATO status quo; that permits it to cope with uncertainty and instability without primary reliance on traditional military force; and that encourages unprecedented levels of cooperation and sharing with all of Europe, including the Soviet Union.

The task will not be as straightforward as seemed possible in the first phase of euphoria at the ending of the Cold War. The United States was then acknowledged as the only true superpower, that is, the only state with economic and military capabilities that allow a global political reach; the Gulf War experience seemed positive proof. Yet to many the United States seems less able and clearly less willing to do much of what it has done in the past: to take up a comprehensive agenda toward the new world order proclaimed by

This essay draws on the research and conclusions also presented in Catherine McArdle Kelleher, "U.S. Foreign Policy and Europe: 1990–2000," *The Brookings Review* (Fall 1990), pp. 4–10.

the Bush administration. Analysts of the "declinist" school argue that
this results from past military "overstretch"—from inattention to the
central requirements of international economic competitiveness.[1]
Others proclaim—more softly perhaps than before the Iraq war—the
sharply declining significance of military power and the irresistible
rise of the new economic superpowers, Europe and Japan. Indeed,
there are increasing numbers of Americans—both on the left and
the right—who now call for a "Come Home America" strategy re-
plete with new forms of isolationism and new claims that the primary national agenda is domestic social and economic reform. In
security as in economic policy, Europe not only can do well on its
own but must now do so.

The argument of this chapter is that any new definition of American national interests and security requirements will include continuing American involvement in the security of Europe—in the
safeguarding of the European peace order the United States has done
so much to create. Security roles and missions will surely be transformed; standing military presence as a guarantee of U.S. support
will no longer necessarily be a critical indicator. There are and will
be new opportunities and new ways for the United States to build
on its past achievements and to exploit its continuing economic and
military power. Its skills at devising cooperative solutions and at
moving toward a cooperative international order, its willingness to
take risks to foster crisis containment and indeed crisis prevention,
will be even more important in securing Europe in the future than
they have been in the past.

What will be required, however, are fundamental changes in
American security policy and practice. Most basic of all will be
changes in the ways in which the United States will view Europe
and will share with its European allies in cooperative decisions
about security for Europe and worldwide. Of almost equal importance will be reconsideration of the domestic preconditions of
American foreign policy behavior—budgetary, bureaucratic, and political.

THE POSTWAR POLICY CONTEXT

America's perspective on Europe over the past forty-five years,
though now being overturned, still sheds light on the ways in which
the United States will view Europe over the next several decades.
At least it helps to clarify the questions to be asked now. The
answers may come later.

One of the most novel aspects of the postwar revolution in American foreign policy was the definition of Europe as somehow immutably part of the American security identity. At one level, to the wartime policy elite American postwar national interests seemed best served by a liberal international order and large free trade zones and by the maintenance of a favorable balance of power in Europe and on the rimland of Asia, anchored by the old democracies and by the reformed Germany and Japan. But the truly revolutionary changes came not in the definition of traditional national interest but in the elite and popular definition of the American security identity. In contrast to the stark separationist views of the 1920s and 1930s, American leaders and constituencies alike came with increasing intensity to view Europeans as "most like us," a people to be defended as we defend ourselves, a kindred people with whom to share the benefits and the risks of the international order established after the defeat of fascism. It was, of course, only Western Europe—NATO Europe plus a few respectable others—that was at issue. Eastern Europe largely drifted from view; the Soviet Union after the Czech coup and the Berlin blockade of 1948 was again consigned to the outer darkness.

It is this sense of the United States and Europe as being kindred and incorporated that is now subject to the greatest pressures for change. The problem is not the revolutionary changes in Eastern Europe, the potential of a unified Germany, or the overblown debate about responsibilities and roles in the Iraq action. For most policy elites and the broad public, the general identity of American and European interests is still intact; in every vital area, cooperation still far outweighs conflict and continuing mutual irritation. But emerging from American and European discussions is a powerful new sense of inevitable Atlantic disengagement, of European identity, and eventual American autarky. For certain critical groups, the basic Atlantic consensus and long-term European-American cooperation no longer seem to be as relevant or compelling conceptions for the future.

At issue are three fundamental postwar American images of Europe, perceptions that served as both good and real reasons for Europe to be the central focus of postwar American security policy. The first and dominant perception was of Europe as the cockpit of history— site of the postwar political and ideological struggle with the Soviet Union. The security of a devastated Europe from both internal subversion and external pressure became the acid test of America's determination to make the world truly safe for democracy. The existence of a Europe "like us" was a precondition to the establishment of a favorable international order based on the principles of the Atlantic Charter of 1941, especially after hopes for the United Nations system froze in the face of East-West rivalry. In the language of Bretton Woods, democratic, capitalist European systems, tied inextricably to an international economic order led by the United States, were ultimately in America's best interest. The cost of postwar European reconstruction was high, but from this perspective the Marshall Plan was simply the down payment on a future of common benefit and continuing American growth.

Another part of Europe's price was a strategy involving both containment for the Soviet Union and extension of an American security guarantee of Western Europe. The American military guarantee provided the shield behind which those "like us" could restore and then maintain functioning political systems that would avoid the ideological quarrels and fatal social divisions that led to the triumph of fascism. Soviet military strength was overwhelming, whatever the Soviet intention. American nuclear weapons balanced, first, Soviet conventional numbers and, then, Soviet nuclear forces themselves. But, for the original doctrine of containment, the critical need was reassurance against political pressure.

The essential factor was continued American military superiority and increasingly, for many, a direct permanent military presence in Europe so that Americans would not have "to fight their way back again." For much of the 1950s, most Americans expected that European reconstruction would mean the eventual withdrawal of American forces. But from the second Berlin crisis onward, a continuing American presence and the visible deployment of American nuclear weapons for the defense of Europe were defined by successive American administrations and by all West European governing elites except the French as an absolute sine qua non—the irreplaceable component without which the European security system and the European peace order would not hold.

A central secondary task was the reform and then rehabilitation of the West Germans in ways that ensured both future stability in the European balance and the maximum use of German resources in deterrence and defense. Most Americans had more confidence than Europeans about relying immediately on German ingenuity and industriousness once the initial horrors of World War II had passed. German participation in the defense of the West was "natural" so long as an integrated framework could be constructed against a revival of German militarism. The struggle for German hearts and minds—first against the legacy of nazism and then against Soviet blandishment—was seen as the centerpiece of American efforts to spread democracy and create an international (or at least free world) system favorable to basic American values.

Through the 1960s, European and American interests continued to be seen as congruent, if not identical, over both the long and short haul. Atlantic defense cooperation and economic coordination were seen as reflecting the basic identity of interests among democratic industrial states. Détente made the necessary connection between economic interests and containment less obvious during the 1970s. The struggles during the 1980s over first the gas pipeline issue and then the intermediate-range nuclear forces (INF) also tested the relationship. Yet both the deployment and the agreement to eliminate INF were seen in Washington at least as demonstrating the basic rightness and resolve of the Atlantic strategy. Tough decisions had been taken and implemented; the Soviet Union had won neither its games in Europe nor the opportunity, probably, to return to the field.

The second significant American perspective on postwar Europe was the necessity of "doing it right," of creating within Western Europe a zone of peace. Having twice rescued Europe from chaos and conflict of its own making, this time the United States would ensure that peacemaking worked: that the Europe it had twice restored with its expeditionary forces would be rebuilt on a stable democratic and regional basis.

Central to this perspective was the concept of a regional security system. The immediate task was to mobilize European resources against the Soviet Union and to provide for German rearmament. Yet, for at least the first postwar decade, a goal of almost equal importance was the organization of a lasting regional balance, designed within the boundaries of the collective self-defense guarantees by the UN Charter's Article 51. The overwhelming preference of policymakers, liberal and conservative alike, was a Europe strong enough and united enough to organize its own defenses, with the U.S. role decreasing to one of general leadership, especially in nuclear matters, and of an emergency fire brigade. Washington's image of which European organization would be most appropriate changed with European events. For John Foster Dulles and Dwight Eisenhower, the dominant image was a European Defense Community (EDC), a security organization along the lines of the Coal and Steel Community, an image that lingered even after the 1954 defeat of the EDC treaty. But by the early 1960s there was increasing American support for the possibilities of a second pillar within a looser NATO or even an incipient Franco-German bargain that would downplay differences and smooth both the European balance and the transatlantic bargain.

After the mid-1960s and France's withdrawal from the alliance, the unity of NATO and a direct transatlantic partnership were seen as the only right answer. The health of the alliance and the loyalty of the national members became litmus tests for how well Europe's interwar problems of stability and cooperation had been resolved. The alliance was not perfect. It called for continuing American sacrifices in the interest of European security that were never reciprocated or appreciated. In the eyes of Congress, NATO clearly needed a new system of burden sharing and better consultation on American strategic preferences. But for diplomats and military officers alike, it was a working organization, of great value for concerting policies in ways that bilateral channels did not allow and with a military structure of impressive deterrent strength.

Increasingly, support for NATO in its existing form became American political orthodoxy. Critics were mainly liberals who, together with scattered conservative leaders, questioned the need for continuing massive American involvement on behalf of a rich Europe and the need for the United States to play global policeman, especially in a Europe strong enough to fight for its own interests. Liberals also worried that the United States had been trapped into answering the wrong questions in its concern for stability and the European balance. Defining the primary task of U.S. foreign policy as the avoidance of nuclear war and the stabilizing of relations with the Soviet Union, these critics argued that NATO was a critical significant bond but that it was neither paramount nor immutable in the calculation of American, or even European, interests. The approach was now globalist, with NATO only one of many instruments. But through the late 1980s, NATO remained the testing stone of the European-American relationship and the emphasis on common military security—the major transatlantic "business" in the understanding of most Americans.

The last American image was of a democratic Europe as a global partner, taking and required to take an active role in the creation of international order and the maintenance of stability. A Europe "like us" could not be left to self-absorption or narrow protectionism, whether its considerations were maintaining colonial empires or remaining within a self-satisfied domestic economic environment. The overriding goal must be to serve what the United States saw as the general Western interest. Over time, the specific standards set for European involvement or openness varied, the issues ranging from participation in Vietnam and arms sales to restrictive preferential trading and investment policies. The forum was most often the Middle East but also Latin America, Africa, and Southeast Asia.

But consistently from the 1950s through the 1980s the charge was the same: The Europeans were insular, recalcitrant, stingy, or soft—and always in the rear.

THE PRESENT POLICY CONTEXT:
AN EVOLVING EUROPE

Looking to the future in American-European security relationships is still chancy; it seems easier to specify the general outcome of this transition period than the precise route from here to there. It is already clear that the new world order with which the United States will have to deal, and the new Europe in which it should be involved, will resist the assumptions and easy habits of leadership developed by past Washingtons. Whether organized as an extended European Community, as a pan-Europe spanning what was once East, West, or neutral, or as something in between, Europe will demand its own identity. It may well have done so even without the end of the Cold War, once the promise of Europe 1992 was fully developed. But with the events of 1989 and 1990, there is no turning back. There is a new European identity in the process of being created, one in which there will be new borders of identity and new partnerships that will be at least as important as those we have seen so far in either the transatlantic sphere or indeed in Western Europe. In the initial stages of this process, the United States will play a critical role, will be "present at the creation."[2] But over time, its central role will diminish and its leadership mute into partnership—the result of European priorities, congressional action, or both.

If present patterns hold, the new Europe will have increasingly lower security requirements, at least as traditionally defined. Although still a nuclear superpower, the Soviet Union will be more of a regional great power in economics and politics, increasingly anxious to have a major part in the European economic and political game. Its future as a unitary state is still uncertain; so too the eventual disposition of its military forces and nuclear weapons. But two conclusions seem certain. The Soviet East European security zone is gone forever; it could only be regained at the cost of war. Moreover, the most likely outcome is a downward spiral rather than a policy of a hostile regeneration—a spiral marked by continuing domestic economic difficulties and political fragmentation. The pressures for lower military budgets and lower standing forces, no matter who is in power, are probably inescapable. To hedge against these events—to counter the risks of ethnic violence and mass population movements—European states will continue to maintain military forces but at levels and with structures far more like those of the late nineteenth century than those of the last forty years.

Perhaps the most difficult part of this adjustment for the United States will be the change to a new relationship with the Federal Republic of Germany, the key actor in all the future European circles. The postwar German-American relationship has gone through a number of phases: Germany as pupil, Germany as key NATO ally, and Germany as America's strategic partner in the ending of the Cold War. The present transition seems to allow for a confusing range of possible outcomes: the result of German self-absorption with the burdens of unification, the successful tactical moves by American and NATO officials in transforming the old alliance structures, and the division of European opinion about the appropriate European security architecture for the short term. The implications of the Gulf War, the testing points of the Yugoslav crisis, the fate of the Gorbachev reforms and the preservation of the Soviet Union—these are the items dominating the short-term agenda and absorbing attention and emotion.

But the end of the Cold War and German unification unmistakably signal the end of imposed political constraints on Germany and most of postwar German security dependency. The Federal Republic will increasingly be a more "ordinary country,"[3] a more powerful middle power than most, with a unique historical burden, but a state whose evolution will probably be even less affected by American choices and preferences than the assertive Federal Republic of the 1980s. A united Germany will always have a more broadly defined security agenda, a more demanding, confident tone, and a far more critical approach to the past bargains struck with the United States and its West European partners. It has stronger political and economic interests in stabilizing Eastern Europe—if only to guard against migrations westward. As of now it has a special relationship with the Soviet Union—as broker, guarantor, and as particular interlocutor. This will be true at least until 1994 or 1995, when Soviet troops are withdrawn from German soil, and probably beyond.

From Washington's view, Germany's security needs and those of Europe as a whole will be dealt with by a group of institutions—several European (the EC, the WEU, the CSCE) but with NATO still retaining core functions.[4] The American and German precondition for agreement on unification in the "2 + 4" talks was NATO membership for all of Germany and the retention of significant military forces to a present maximum of 370,000 troops.[5] Ultimately, acceptance by the Soviet Union as well as Britain and France affirms the broad consensus on the utility of the transatlantic framework and the need for a continued American guarantee, especially for Germany.

Less well appreciated throughout Washington, however, is the fact that German unity has itself transformed NATO. It is reflected as well by NATO's London Summit declaration of 1990[6] or the NATO Strategy review[7] as by particular articles in the German-Soviet agreements of 1990 or the specifics of the nonnuclear, no-foreign-troops status of the five new German states. There are changes in personnel (fewer standing forces even as a ceiling, a changing command structure, perhaps a German supreme commander for NATO) as well as in strategy (the shift from larger active forces and static forward defense at the inner-German border to smaller, highly mobile, multinational units and a policy of force regeneration should unlikely war threaten). There will be far fewer, if any, nuclear weapons on German soil in the future, given the expressed preferences of both East and West Germans. And over the next decade, NATO forces stationed in Germany will unquestionably shrink, if not reach the vanishing point—with an American contingent of 75,000 to 100,000 troops (if any at all) by the end of the 1990s now widely discussed.[8]

The most important transformation, not yet visible, will go to the heart of the basic American assumptions and basic patterns of behavior that have constituted the American conception of NATO over the past four decades. To draw an analogy from nineteenth-century diplomacy: The United States and indeed the NATO organization itself will take on much more the role of guarantors and reinsurers. Moreover, as the European Community assumes a defense identity, Americans—whether as officials, political elites, or even political parties—will find themselves tied to security concerns and arrangements in Europe by interest and convenience but less by day-to-day necessity. They will have interests to be defended but they will not be the organizers or even be necessarily central to the security enterprise. Clearly, too, the kinds of military details that have been the obsessive concern of successive Washingtons—the particular balances to be struck and the characteristics of particular force structures—will simply be less important.

Moreover, Europeans will see the contribution of military security to overall stability as only equal to, perhaps even less critical than, those of economic reconstruction and expansion, especially vis-à-vis Eastern Europe. Economic status and competitiveness will be the measure of day-to-day European power, with an expanded Germany as the keystone of the community, even if the EC increases its direct membership (Austria and perhaps Sweden in this decade) or its associations with the EFTA states and Eastern Europe. Without a regularized link to this community that goes beyond NATO, the United States will find itself more of an outsider—more dependent on the intervention and assistance of others for access than at any time in the postwar period. And without full involvement in the redevelopment and reshaping of the East European economies, Washington may find its policy preferences far less relevant to the daily policy concerns of an emerging German economic superpower or a European economic "pole" that is even more competitive.

One aspect of the new Europe that Americans will find rewarding will be the increasing emphasis placed on democratic rule as the critical standard for bilateral and multilateral relationships. The new emphasis will emerge not only because of the guarantees of stability and noninterference that democracies generally provide but also because the most powerful states—Germany, the EC members, and the United States itself—believe that democratic rule will best safeguard their interests. Democratization may well prove a tough, exclusionary test for the new Europe. Much of the Balkans will become marginal; a military-dominated Greece or Turkey will be consigned to secondary European status. If the Soviet Union or a Soviet republic clings to bureaucratically authoritarian structures or an East European country returns to the popular authoritarianism of the 1930s, it will have less status and perhaps ultimately a lesser share in the European game.

For much of this next decade, the United States will be struggling to understand and to adapt its relationship to a Europe that we (Americans) define as only somewhat like "us." In this new relationship there will be a variety of organizations and structures charged with the preservation of security that have overlapping responsibilities, ambitions, and memberships. Almost certainly included will be a European Community with expanded powers, functions, and membership and with a special defense identity. There may well be a traditional NATO viable not only as a core framework for a limited transitional phase but also as the loosely structured reflection of a continuing transatlantic "security community."[9] There may also be a looser, less central CSCE as an overarching umbrella organization to facilitate associations with Eastern Europe but also with specific functions for arms control, crisis prevention, and perhaps peacekeeping. Most but not all will involve roles for the United States, sometimes equal, sometimes secondary. The meshing of these various organizational activities and the political and economic compromises they represent will be the major challenge of the second half of the 1990s.

EUROPEAN SECURITY
AND AMERICAN NATIONAL INTEREST

In this period of transition in American-European relations, it is worthwhile to distinguish between fundamental U.S. foreign policy interests to be preserved and shorter-run goals at stake in the evolution of new cooperative security structures between the United States and Europe. From the vantage point of 1991, there seem four basic American interests at stake in the guaranteeing of Europe's security that, at a minimum, allow identification of future changes that are risk-laden or politically troublesome.

First, it remains in the basic interest of the United States that the present zone of economic and political peace in Europe be maintained and expanded. At stake is the pattern of consistent, transparent, peaceful relationships that have prevailed among political units in Western Europe since 1949. The doctrine of containment was fundamentally designed to safeguard these new patterns of European interaction against Soviet military but especially political pressure. It was these patterns that the United States believed and still believes are most conducive both to political stability and to economic prosperity in Europe and throughout the rest of the world.

The evolution of this zone of peace does not itself provide for the inevitability of either NATO or the European Community in its present structural configuration. But it does provide strong incentives to preserve them at least as transitional structures. And any new European framework must incorporate guarantees to safeguard and extend their principal outcomes—regular, cooperative, open relations within overarching multilateral structures charged with political, economic, and military security. Moreover, these structures are to be viewed by national electorates as normal, predictable, and preferable to past competition and conflict—or to future instability or fragmentation.

Maintaining this zone is in the basic interest of the United States whatever the ultimate European framework. If the new Europe is a more potent economic competitor or far less tied to U.S. security guarantees, a Europe open to the free flow of trade and ideas is still a critical cornerstone in the type of international political order that the United States requires in the 1990s—perhaps even more than it did in 1945. And if economic competition grows between Europe,

Japan, and the United States into the twenty-first century, the existence of structures that safeguard a free economic zone will be of even greater significance for U.S. interests.

The second basic interest is to preserve for the United States a role vis-à-vis all basic European players, a role not necessarily of the same form or scope but one actively involved in European security. Whatever its eventual scope, American involvement must not be dependent on the goodwill of any single European partner, whether Germany or any other "strategic" ally. Also, despite the present Washington stress on NATO's preservation, it is not a basic American interest to cling to any particular structure much less to an emphasis on purely military cooperation to the detriment or exclusion of far more important economic and political coordination and policy development. To ensure American access across the spectrum of European policy areas, the United States must not react defensively to the evolution of a European defense identity within the community or stand back from new forms of cooperation with Eastern Europe. Instead it should actively participate in their creation. Such a strategy is both a hedge against the future and an opportunity to underline the continuing stake the United States has in Europe and in a peaceful European order.

Carrying out this strategy requires flexibility and a critical reeducation of American policymakers and publics about possible European outcomes. The American postwar preference has been for decisionmaking in Washington to flow through clear-cut and mutually reinforcing channels of influence. Typically the United States has relied on strong, semiexclusive partnerships, first with Britain and then with the Federal Republic; strong multilateral organizations of friendly major actors, such as the G-7 group; and well-defined structures for multilateral diplomacy and integrated functional action—principally NATO but also the Coordinating Committee for Multilateral Export Controls (COCOM) and the International Monetary Fund. At best, the United States must strive now for multiple channels of influence but without the assurance either of a continuing commanding role or of easy policy coordination. To do this with grace will be hard; to do it effectively, still harder.

However, even a minimum American security role in Europe should be a positive factor, given both enormous American assets and newfound flexibility. In the short run, the United States will be the primary reassurer of a new Germany against a gathering of its rivals; it will also provide the balance wheel that all Europeans, East and West, seem to want for now. For the longer term, the United States may be more an available partner, an honest broker, and, only occasionally, a makeweight in a German-led Europe or a hedge against residual threats of ethnic unrest, Soviet reversals, or political collapse in Eastern Europe or, more likely, the Soviet Union.

The third fundamental interest lies in the orderly political transition of both united Germany and the Soviet Union to their new European roles. This must be a primary goal for the United States, even though American efforts will be neither exclusive nor determining. To many, American images of Europe have always been too pro-Bonn or German-centric. But it is now more essential than ever that the United States reinforce a democratic Germany—the new kind of democratic Germany—as the new king of democratic as well as economic Europe. A continuing American military presence, so long as it remains wanted by the Germans and other Europeans, will stay useful. And American participation, on more equitable terms and in more cooperating or coordinating modes, will be essential.

This may well not be a decade of great calm in German-American relations as the dialogues between Washington and Bonn on the Gulf War, on aid for Gorbachev, and on Yugoslavia have already shown. Germany will undoubtedly be more self-absorbed with unification tasks than Washington would prefer; less willing (and able) to contribute to what Washington defines as the transatlantic common good; and more determined to stabilize its Eastern neighbors, whatever America's views. Mutual irritations will grow, and there will be many temptations to rehearse the German past to constrain the German future. But the United States will still have a unique fostering role to play despite policy differences and diverging areas of primary economic commitment. The United States may have to do for Germany what Britain did for the United States in the late nineteenth century—help without obvious support or direct interference, consult at the grand level with tolerance and flexibility for the inevitable clashes and irritations. And it should do so gladly—and for its own long-run benefit.

The focus of the U.S.-Soviet relationship will be far less defined and subject to far more domestic debate than the tie with Bonn. Given budget deficits, caution, and lingering ideologies, Washington will probably play a less direct role in Soviet economic and political restructuring, whether reform or decentralization, than will Germany and the other major West European states. It will certainly play a smaller direct role in the short run in democratizing Eastern Europe. U.S. reluctance to be actively involved reflects both present economic limitations and the willingness for now to define European interests in these areas as primary. But there is also considerable

American ambivalence to be resolved about the limits of European involvement and the impact this should be allowed to have on American commitments and interests.[10]

As for the Soviet role, the United States should play a facilitating, structuring part in involving even a rump Soviet Union in Europe, especially in all-European security and economic arrangements. It is not in the U.S. strategic interest to allow, much less encourage, the marginalization of the Soviet Union in European or global affairs. Rather, the United States should actively support Soviet participation in multilateral solutions to pressing regional problems ranging from environmental degradation to ethnic unrest to the safety of remaining nuclear weapons. It should also promote Soviet acceptance of the standards of behavior, responsibility, and internal political compromise that have prevailed in Western Europe since the late 1950s. And in the short run the United States can provide legitimacy for the constraints on military capabilities that affect European security arrangements that the Soviet Union (and the United States) will have to accept.

The fourth basic American interest posits guaranteed political and economic access with Europe and to Europe. This not only reflects America's own security and economic needs but also represents an exercise of influence on behalf of the have-nots in Europe and throughout the rest of the world. The principal economic gatekeepers will clearly be European—the community, the deutsche mark bloc, or Germany itself. At a minimum, however, there should be positive American encouragement against European protectionism and excessive Eurocentric self-absorption. At a maximum, it might involve the development of joint American-European ventures in the interest of specific development goals, requirements of regional security, or hedges against environmental dangers. At the core will be the education of the democratic electorate, American and European, about cooperative international structures, and a recasting of the limits and obligations of state sovereignty and economic power.

SHORT-RANGE AMERICAN SECURITY GOALS

To fulfill these long-term interests there must also be shorter-range American security goals. Perhaps the most obvious is the shift to far lower levels of military deployment and preparedness over the next four to five years. A zero-force level has much support in Congress as well as on the European left. However, without serious consideration of why military force is to be maintained at all, such actions now seem premature and perhaps counterproductive. Certainly a continuing American military presence, acceptable both to Europeans and to the United States, has strategic meaning as well as political significance.

A related American goal should be to demonstrate a willingness to reexamine and to accept new levels of partnership critique on all aspects of NATO doctrine and force structure. One obvious example before us is the debate that concerns the future of air-launched, short-range nuclear forces (e.g., TASM [tactical anti-shortrange missiles]). Bush administration policy seems destined to repeat all the mistakes of the INF and SNF (shortrange nuclear forces) crises by its insistence on the modernization of present systems but without direct exploration of formal parallel arms control.[11] The logic of follow-on systems has been discussed and revealed to be complex; making this a test of European loyalty or of American influence is simply unnecessary. Burden and risk sharing and their utilities need to be looked at in new ways in the post-Cold War international system.

The third policy, and perhaps a harder policy than Washington now realizes, is support for both the creation and the tolerance of new organizational overlaps regarding security responsibilities in Europe and throughout the world. NATO has been so relatively easy for the United States for so long that there are many who confuse its continued existence in its present form with the defense of Western civilization. But the Bush administration has now said that it expects change and will adapt to it, particularly in terms of a Europeanization not only of NATO but of European security as well.[12] Here perhaps the immediate litmus test will be the American policy toward CSCE and the attempt to develop new cooperative integrative structures that provide assurance for the new East European democracies and what will become of the Soviet Union. There will also have to be more support for a wide-ranging exploration within the community about the scope and pace of the new European defense identity; attempts to insist on NATO loyalty per se will be clearly counterproductive.

Last is the question that is perhaps most troublesome in the short run: the role to be played by Eastern Europe and the Soviet Union within all European organizations. Here it is in the interest of the United States to increase the levels and indeed the commonality of the cooperative functions to be assumed by these nations. Everything from a pan-European civilian/military air traffic control system to a joint expansion of the new verification and crisis prevention agencies should be encouraged. The goals should be to provide direct reassurance, to strengthen democratic, collaborative experience, to encourage transparency, and, perhaps most of all, to allow a deepening of ties and behaviors that will make later direct integration more predictable and more stabilizing for publics and elites.

AMERICAN DOMESTIC GOALS TO SUPPORT A NEW POLICY TOWARD EUROPE

All of this will come at a price, and the price probably will be paid most directly within American domestic politics. Probably the first "cost" will turn on the willingness of various parts of the American political spectrum not to invent a new devil or substitute a new set of enemies for the enemy now gone. The level of Japan bashing over the past two years, and the incipient level of German bashing, for example, will simply have to go away. And continuing American skepticism about collective security should fade before more debate begins about the relative benefits of unilateral or allied action versus the security to be gained now through new international cooperative arrangements. The answer will almost surely not focus on a single institution or set of arrangements but will probably also suggest far more restricted areas for unilateral decision or action.

A second and more painful price, both in the short term and in the long term, is the need to adjust domestic economic policies to the new international framework. Whether exhibited in the budget or in the way in which the economy is organized and run, this adjustment requires not just the acceptance of normal international burdens but also a continuing commitment against the easy substitution of international sacrifice for domestic political advantage. "Beggar-my-neighbor" economic policies and unilateral American decisions assigning security costs and risks to others are both unacceptable. Even less justifiable will be a retreat into protective neoisolationism or the mindless withdrawal of forces in the putative interest of fiscal savings and the politically driven retention of domestic bases.

Third is the need for a new American understanding of the role of the military budget itself and of defense investment in a time of both cold peace and pent-up domestic social demand. The pressure for a peace dividend, for a restructuring of forces, and risks to acknowledge the changed political environment will be irresistible. But it will not be appropriate now to neglect basic requirements needed to do long-term force regeneration in the case of a renewed major military threat in Europe; to assure minimum deterrence in both the conventional and nuclear arena; or to insure crisis prevention and crisis containment at Europe's periphery, in the Middle East, or around the world. How to meet both goals is a debate that has been long postponed, and it is one that the United States will enter with great reluctance but nonetheless with great urgency.

Perhaps the most difficult domestic challenge of all will be to revive and renew the arguments, first heard from 1945 to 1947 and often cynically dismissed thereafter, about the prospects of a world without war, the opportunities to, in fact, spread the blessings of democracy so recently defended and the need to help extend not just military security but economic prosperity and a set of basic political rights to all peoples. How do we translate this charge, first set forth in the Atlantic Charter by Franklin Roosevelt and Winston Churchill, into the present American political agenda? What kind of willingness will there now be to envision concepts of cooperative security and eventually a set of regional security arrangements or even a worldwide security system? It is a challenge to which the American political system is unaccustomed and for which it is relatively unqualified. It deals best with things in the margin, issues that are incremental, things that are direct and involve pragmatic decision. But far more than in any present European parliamentary system, the American political establishment has occasionally responded to "big ideas" with great flexibility and with great speed and has discerned that there are fundamental national interests to be served in the creation of benefits of liberty that others can share. Perhaps their realization is still possible at the end of this Cold War, just as in the period from 1945 to 1949.

CONCLUSION

Much can derail the fundamental assumptions here about the future of American-European relations in the 1990s. Developments in the Soviet Union are the obvious wild card. The critical obstacles may be the effects of a rapidly and radically fragmenting Soviet Union and the induction of a chain reaction along its periphery. As the Yugoslav crisis shows, the stubborn hatreds of Balkan ethnic politics still survive. There is still room in the short run for British and French intransigence about their national nuclear status and for the collapse of the hopeful democracies in Eastern Europe in the face of economic failures and political vacillation. German unification will run myriad risks, not the least of which is the short-run education and incorporation of a xenophobic East German population that, of historical necessity, has a self-centered economic agenda and an immature political sense. There is always the possibility, but not the probability, of American neoisolationism. And there is no guarantee that Europe itself will not stall at the level of a customs union or will be able to overcome the temptations of renationalization, whether economic, political, or military.

But there is one clear conclusion. The United States faces a decade of great challenge and opportunity to cooperate in, not create, a new Europe. It will require immense moderation and restraint, a recasting of many of the truisms and lessons of prewar European-American relations, and a reformulation of some, but not all, of the images of Europe that the United States has developed since 1945. The United States will have to adjust to the new economic competition with Europe (and Japan) with greater equanimity than it has shown until now and downgrade the significance of military power in U.S. foreign policy generally and with regard to Europe in particular. It will also have to steadfastly insist on its continuing stake in the security of an evolving Europe, a Europe begun in its own image and now able to assume new responsibilities in the peaceful international order that is now possible to achieve.

NOTES

1. For a more comprehensive description and explication of these arguments, see Catherine M. Kelleher, "The Changing Currency of Power: The Future of U.S. Influence in Western Europe and North-East Asia," International Institute of Strategic Studies, ed., *America's Role in a Changing World,* Adelphi Paper No. 256 (Winter 1990/1991).

2. See Dean Acheson, *Present at the Creation: My Years in the State Department* (New York: Norton 1969).

3. The "ordinariness" is to be understood in the same sense as Richard Rosecrance's classic definition in his *America as an Ordinary Country* (Ithaca: Cornell University Press 1976).

4. See here the development of American foreign policy on this issue reflected in two remarkable speeches on America and Europe, given by Secretary of State James A. Baker III in Berlin. The first was "A New Europe, a New Atlanticism: Architecture for a New Era," on December 12, 1989, just after the Wall's fall (Department of State, *Current Policy,* no. 1233 [1989]), and the second was given on June 18, 1991, to the Aspen Institute Berlin, "The Euro-Atlantic Architecture: From West to East," Department of State, press release, June 18, 1991.

5. For details of the American and German negotiating positions in the "2 + 4" talks, see Steven Szabo's forthcoming book on German unification

and the various participant/eyewitness accounts to be published jointly by the American Institute for Contemporary German Studies and the School of Advanced International Studies, Johns Hopkins University. An interesting comparative view is presented by Wolfgang Pfeiler in "Die Viermächte-Option als Instrument sowjetischer Deutschlandpolitik," *Study* 25/1991, Forschungsinstitut der Konrad-Adenauer-Stiftung, Sankt Augustin, Federal Republic of Germany.

6. NATO, "London Declaration on a Transformed North Atlantic Alliance," issued by the heads of state and government participating in the meeting of the North Atlantic Council in London on July 5–6, 1990, in *NATO Review* 38, no. 4 (August 1990), pp. 32–33.

7. See for details "The Alliance's New Strategic Concept," agreed by the heads of state and government participating in the meeting of the North Atlantic Council in Rome on November 7–8, 1991, in *NATO Press Service,* Press Communique S-1(91)85, November 7, 1991.

8. Compare here the discussion of former NATO SACEUR general Andrew J. Goodpaster (U.S., retired) in several occasional papers published by the Atlantic Council, Washington: "Gorbachev and the Future of East-West Security: A Response for the Mid-Term," of April 1989; and "New Priorities for U.S. Security: Military Needs and Tasks in a Time of Change," of June 1991.

9. This would be in the sense of the use of the term "security community" by Karl W. Deutsch, Sidney A. Burrel, Robert A. Kann, Maurice Lee, Jr., Martin Lichtermann, Raymond E. Lindren, Francis L. Loewenheim, Richard W. Van Wagenen, *Political Community and the North Atlantic Area: International Organization in the Light of Historical Experience* (Princeton: Princeton University Press 1957).

10. This is the essence of the American-European debate of winter 1991 over the so-called Bartholomew letter. According to interview reports, the letter sent to all NATO governments in the EC was an American attempt to draw explicit future limits on European non-NATO actions. It reportedly grew out of White House and Pentagon fears that in the foreseeable future a European political or security grouping might take actions that would result in NATO involvement in Eastern Europe without prior alliance decision or might lead to commitments vis-à-vis other non-NATO states (especially in Europe but theoretically outside of Europe as well) without full alliance consultation beforehand. A more balanced effort toward the same end led to the Genscher-Baker communique delineating the four major goals of future American-European security efforts issued in Washington in April 1991. These were later incorporated into the final communique of the Copenhagen meeting of the NATO Council in June 1991.

11. See for details my summary article "Short-Range Nuclear Weapons: What Future in Europe?" *Arms Control Today* (January/February 1991).

12. See Baker's June 1991 Berlin speech, Note 4.

About the Book
and Editors

What will the new world order look like—a tripole, a layer cake, a concert hall? Will Europe and the United States continue in their tradition of interdependence and admiration or emerge as economic rivals, political strangers, and cultural antipodes as the rest of the world—notably Japan—moves forward?

These are just some of the questions explored within this unusual volume. No matter how the questions may be resolved, the transatlantic relationship is in flux, and new roles, responsibilities, and capacities are being defined. Here, leading scholars converge on the prospects for change in U.S.-European relations and offer new insights into the theory and practice of international relations in a reconfigured world.

Each original essay addresses a set of common themes central to the study of the new global order: causes and consequences of change; balance versus currencies of power; international institutions; conflict versus cooperation; winners versus losers; foreign versus domestic priorities; new roles and policy options. At the same time, each essay is distinguished by the particular theoretical perspective of its author, and all themes and theories are drawn together in a powerful introduction by the international editorial team.

Helga Haftendorn is professor of political science and international relations and director of the Institute for Transatlantic Foreign and Security Policy Studies at the Free University of Berlin. *Christian Tuschhoff* is a senior research fellow at the Institute for Transatlantic Foreign and Security Policy Studies.

About the Contributors

Helga Haftendorn, professor of political science and international relations, Free University of Berlin, and director, Institute for Transatlantic Foreign and Security Policy Studies, Free University of Berlin. Publications (among others): *Security and Detente: Conflicting Priorities in German Foreign Policy* (1985); "The Security Puzzle: Theory-Building and Discipline-Building in International Security," *International Studies Quarterly* 35, no. 1 (March 1991), pp. 3–17.

Stanley Hoffmann, Douglas Dillon Professor, Harvard University, and director, Center for European Studies, Harvard University. Publications (among others): *Gulliver's Troubles, or the Setting of American Foreign Policy* (1968); *Janus and Minerva: Essays in Theory and Practice of International Politics* (Westview Press, 1987).

Peter J. Katzenstein, Walter S. Carpenter, Jr., Professor of International Studies, Cornell University, Ithaca, N.Y. Publications (among others): *Small States in World Markets: Industrial Policy in Europe* (1985); editor, *Industry and Politics in West Germany: Toward the Third Republic* (1989).

Catherine McArdle Kelleher, professor of public policy and director, Center for International Security Studies of the School of Public Affairs, University of Maryland; guest professor with the Brookings Institution, Washington, D.C. Publications (among others): *Germany and the Politics of Nuclear Weapons* (1975); "Classical Arms Control in a Revolutionary Future: Europe," *Daedalus* (Winter 1991), pp. 111–131.

Robert O. Keohane, professor of government, Harvard University. Publications (among others): *After Hegemony: Cooperation and Discord in the World Political Economy* (1984); *International Institutions and State Power: Essays in International Relations Theory* (Westview Press, 1989).

Stephen D. Krasner, professor of political science, Stanford University; editor of *International Organization.* Publications (among others): *Structural Conflict: The Third World Against Global Liberalism* (1985); "National Power and Global Communications: Life on the Pareto Frontier," *World Politics* 43, no. 3 (April 1991), pp. 336–366.

Joseph S. Nye, Jr., Ford Foundation Professor of International Security, Harvard University, and director, Center for International Affairs, Harvard University. Publications (among others): *Power and Interdependence* (together with Robert O. Keohane), 2d ed. (1989); *Bound to Lead: The Changing Nature of American Power* (1990).

Robert D. Putnam, Don K. Price Professor of Politics, Kennedy School of Government; professor of government, Faculty of Arts and Sciences, Harvard University. Publications (among others): *Hanging Together: Conflict and Cooperation in the Seven-Power Summits* (together with Nicholas Bayne), rev. and enlarged ed. (1987); "Diplomacy and Domestic Politics: The Logic of Two-Level Games," *International Organization* 42, no. 3 (Summer 1988), pp. 427–460.

Richard N. Rosecrance, professor of political science, University of California–Los Angeles. Publications (among others): *The Rise of the Trading State: Commerce and Conquest in the Modern World* (1986); *America's Economic Resurgence: A Bold New Strategy* (1990).

Christian Tuschhoff, senior research fellow, Institute for Transatlantic Foreign and Security Policy Studies, Free University of Berlin. Publications (among others): *Einstellung und Entscheidung. Perzeptionen im sicherheitspolitischen Entscheidungsprozess der ersten Reagan-Administration, 1981–1984* (1990); "Bringing Back Appeasement: The Case for Umbrella Solution" (together with Raimund Grafe), in Wolfgang Danspeckgruber (ed.), *Emerging Dimensions of European Security* (Westview Press, 1991), pp. 21–46.

Index

Adenauer, Konrad, 111, 114
Adidas (company), 77
Afghanistan, 88
Africa, 97, 98, 106, 152
AIDS (acquired immune deficiency
    syndrome), 93
Airbus, 66
Air-launched short-range nuclear forces,
    161
Albania, 108
Anarchy, 51, 52
Anti-Americanism, 108
Apartheid, 106
APEC. *See* Asia Pacific Economic
    Cooperation Conference
Argentina, 140
Armenia, 111
Arms sales, 8, 61, 65, 152
ASEAN. *See* Association of Southeast
    Asian Nations
Asia, 3, 6, 9, 12, 49, 50, 51, 54, 61, 78, 94,
    97, 98, 105, 106, 108, 111, 119, 120–121,
    123, 125, 137, 142(table), 149, 152
Asian Development Bank, 121
Asia Pacific Economic Cooperation
    Conference (APEC), 121
Association of Southeast Asian Nations
    (ASEAN), 119, 121
Atlantic Alliance, 7, 9, 25, 37, 41, 76, 116,
    151. *See also* North Atlantic Treaty
    Organization
Atlantic Charter (1941), 150, 163
Attali, Jacques, 98
Austria, 121, 133, 134, 138, 156
Autarky, 39, 77, 119, 129
Authoritarian rule, 44

Baker, James, 44, 108, 115, 123
Balance of power, 2, 5–6, 7, 10, 94, 100,
    131, 135, 143, 144(n16), 149
    winners, 12
Balkans, 156, 163
Baltic states, 111, 138
Belorussia, 68
Berlin blockade (1948), 149
Berlin Wall collapse (1989), 69, 111
Bipolarity, 1, 3, 5, 36, 51, 87, 96–97, 106,
    119
Bismarck, Otto von, 69
*Bound to Lead: The Changing Nature of
    American Power* (Nye), 64, 87
Brandt, Willy, 115
Brazil, 140
Bretton Woods, 115, 119, 150. *See also*
    International Monetary Fund; World
    Bank
Brezhnev, Leonid, 88
Brunei, 119
Brussels Article 133 committee (EC), 80
Bulgaria, 38, 39
Burden sharing, 5, 64, 95, 102–103, 162
Bush, George, 29, 56, 57, 65, 73, 74, 77, 92,
    110, 148, 161
Buzan, Barry, 47

Cable News Network (CNN), 110
Cake analogy, 4, 6, 100
Cambodia, 106
Canada, 33, 78, 120–121, 122, 136
Canada-U.S. Free Trade Agreement, 33,
    78, 120–121
Canning, George, 133
Capabilities, distribution of, 3, 4, 6–8, 21,
    22, 26–29, 34–41